W9-AEE-050

Jacqueline Wilson

WHO WROTE THAT?

WHO WROTE THAT?

Jacqueline Wilson

John Bankston

Foreword by
Kyle Zimmer

CHELSEA HOUSE
An Infobase Learning Company

Jacqueline Wilson

Chelsea House
An imprint of Infobase Learning
132 West 31st Street
New York, NY 10001

Library of Congress Cataloging-in-Publication Data
Bankston, John, 1974–
    Jacqueline Wilson / by John Bankston.
        p. cm. — (Who wrote that?)
    Includes bibliographical references and index.
    ISBN 978-1-60413-773-6 (hardcover)
    1. Wilson, Jacqueline—Juvenile literature. 2. Authors, American—20th century—Biography—Juvenile literature. 3. Children's stories—Authorship—Juvenile literature. I. Title.
    PR6073.I46737Z55 2011
    813'.54—dc22
    [B]   2010047679

Chelsea House books are available at special discounts when purchased in bulk quantities for business, associations, institutions, or sales promotions. Please call our Special Sales Department in New York at (212) 967-8800 or (800) 322-8755.

You can find Chelsea House on the World Wide Web at
http://www.infobaselearning.com.

Text design by Keith Trego
Cover design by Alicia Post
Composition by EJB Publishing Services
Cover printed by Yurchak Printing, Landisville, Pa.
Book printed and bound by Yurchak Printing, Landisville, Pa.
Date printed: May 2011
Printed in the United States of America

10 9 8 7 6 5 4 3 2 1

Table of Contents

FOREWORD BY
KYLE ZIMMER
PRESIDENT, FIRST BOOK

HUMANITY IS POWERED by stories. From our earliest days as thinking beings, we employed every available tool to tell each other stories. We danced, drew pictures on the walls of our caves, spoke, and sang. All of this extraordinary effort was designed to entertain, recount the news of the day, explain natural occurrences—and then gradually to build religious and cultural traditions and establish the common bonds and continuity that eventually formed civilizations. Stories are the most powerful force in the universe; they are the primary element that has distinguished our evolutionary path.

Our love of the story has not diminished with time. Enormous segments of societies are devoted to the art of storytelling. Book sales in the United States alone topped $24 billion in 2006; movie studios spend fortunes to create and promote stories; and the news industry is more pervasive in its presence than ever before.

There is no mystery to our fascination. Great stories are magic. They can introduce us to new cultures, or remind us of the nobility and failures of our own, inspire us to greatness or scare us to death; but above all, stories provide human insight on a level that is unavailable through any other source. In fact, stories connect each of us to the rest of humanity not just in our own time, but also throughout history.

This special magic of books is the greatest treasure that we can hand down from generation to generation. In fact, that spark in a child that comes from books became the motivation for the creation of my organization, First Book, a national literacy program with a simple mission: to provide new books to the most disadvantaged children. At present, First Book has been at work in hundreds of communities for over a decade. Every year children in need receive millions of books through our organization and millions more are provided through dedicated literacy institutions across the United States and around the world. In addition, groups of people dedicate themselves tirelessly to working with children to share reading and stories in every imaginable setting from schools to the streets. Of course, this Herculean effort serves many important goals. Literacy translates to productivity and employability in life and many other valid and even essential elements. But at the heart of this movement are people who love stories, love to read, and want desperately to ensure that no one misses the wonderful possibilities that reading provides.

When thinking about the importance of books, there is an overwhelming urge to cite the literary devotion of great minds. Some have written of the magnitude of the importance of literature. Amy Lowell, an American poet, captured the concept when she said, "Books are more than books. They are the life, the very heart and core of ages past, the reason why men lived and worked and died, the essence and quintessence of their lives." Others have spoken of their personal obsession with books, as in Thomas Jefferson's simple statement: "I live for books." But more compelling, perhaps, is the almost instinctive excitement in children for books and stories.

Throughout my years at First Book, I have heard truly extraordinary stories about the power of books in the lives of children. In one case, a homeless child, who had been bounced from one location to another, later resurfaced—and the only possession that he had fought to keep was the book he was given as part of a First Book distribution months earlier. More recently, I met a child who, upon receiving the book he wanted, flashed a big smile and said, "This is my big chance!" These snapshots reveal the true power of books and stories to give hope and change lives.

As these children grow up and continue to develop their love of reading, they will owe a profound debt to those volunteers who reached out to them—a debt that they may repay by reaching out to spark the next generation of readers. But there is a greater debt owed by all of us—a debt to the storytellers, the authors, who have bound us together, inspired our leaders, fueled our civilizations, and helped us put our children to sleep with their heads full of images and ideas.

WHO WROTE THAT? is a series of books dedicated to introducing us to a few of these incredible individuals. While we have almost always honored stories, we have not uniformly honored storytellers. In fact, some of the most important authors have toiled in complete obscurity throughout their lives or have been openly persecuted for the uncomfortable truths that they have laid before us. When confronted with the magnitude of their written work or perhaps the daily grind of our own, we can forget that writers are people. They struggle through the same daily indignities and dental appointments, and they experience the intense joy and bottomless despair that many of us do. Yet somehow they rise above it all to deliver a powerful thread that connects us all. It is a rare honor to have the opportunity that these books provide to share the lives of these extraordinary people. Enjoy.

Children's author Jacqueline Wilson's books have sold more than 25 million copies worldwide. Today, she is among the most-borrowed authors at British libraries.

Teenage Dropout

JACQUELINE AITKEN WAS just 16 when she quit school. She later described her choice to leave the Coombe County Secondary School for Girls in Surrey, England as "quite joyful."

In the beginning, though, joy was in short supply. Her home in Kingston-on-Thames was dominated by an angry father. Her mother still had not found her way in the world. And Jacky was equally directionless. In the early 1960s, opportunities for even well-educated young women were in short supply. Many hoped for a husband to take care of them. Others pursued work in female-dominated professions such as nursing or teaching.

Almost 50 years ago, there were very few women working in higher-paying fields like law and medicine.

With few skills, Jacky could only find work in another field dominated by women. She became a secretary.

The work was tedious. Typing the words of her bosses was not her dream. She did not want to take dictation. She wanted to get paid for her own words. She wanted to become a published writer.

As a little girl, stories provided Jacky an escape from a treacherous home life. "Money was tight," she told the London *Sunday Times*, "but Mum always made sure I had a new book every birthday, Christmas and summer holiday." In between, she took trips to the library. "When I was ten, Mum asked if I could join the adult library because I'd run out of books to read."[1]

Like many early readers, Jacky became a writer. Even before she was finished with children's books, she had written her own. Her first, the fictional saga of the Maggot family, was a mere 21 pages long, but she considered it to be her first novel. Eight years later, she finally had the chance to get paid for what she had been doing for free.

"When I was seventeen," she recalled in an interview with the London *Guardian*, "DC Thomson advertised for material for a big new teenage magazine it was launching, which didn't yet have a name. I began contributing.

"My first article was about what it's like to go to a posh dance and be the poor soul who doesn't get off with a boyfriend. It was done in a jokey style to try and make other girls who'd gone through this embarrassment laugh a little."[2]

Despite her youth, Jacky already had a leg up on many older writers. She had found her "voice"—her own individual style that set her apart from the other submissions. The editors did not care about her age (most writers working for teen magazines are not teenagers). They did not care about her aborted education. They cared about how her first piece's honest humor could connect with their readers.

For the next few months, Jacky worked as a freelancer—meaning that she was paid by the article and was not on staff. Then the editors offered her a full-time job.

The position was in Scotland. For Jacky, putting more than 200 miles (321.8 kilometers) between herself and a miserable home life was an added blessing. In late 1963, she left for Dundee. Unfortunately, a mix-up left her without a room when she arrived. Jackie spent her first night away from home bedded down in a linen closet. Finding a room of her own did not alleviate one unexpected challenge. "I was so homesick I'd go into the Dundee Woolworths just because it smelled like the one near home," she recalled.[3]

Jacky persevered. Instead of working on a magazine for teenage girls, she was assigned to one for women. In an interview, she recalled:

> Because I was quite young, I had to report to the two guys in charge of women's and teenage magazines every Friday.

Did you know...

Along with Jacqueline Wilson, Sandy Denny, considered one of the founders of the British folk rock movement, was also a famous alumna of the Coombe County Secondary School for Girls.

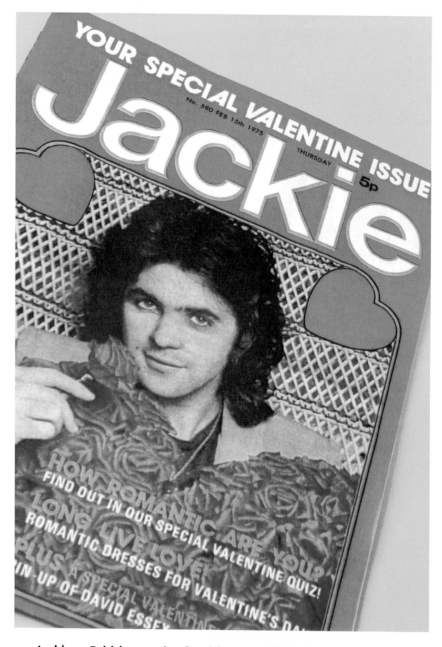

Jackie, *a British magazine for girls, was published by D.C. Thomson & Co. Ltd. of Dundee from January 1964 until its closure in July 1993. Seen here, an issue of the magazine published in February 1975 featuring pop star David Essex on the cover.*

They were called Mr. Cuthbert and Mr. Tate—they sound like a musical team. One day, when I went along, they were chuntering about the new magazine and said, "Did you know it's going to be named after you?" I stared at them blankly, and they said, "Well, you wait and see." Anyway, when the magazine came out in 1964, it was called *Jackie*.[4]

Today, the story that, at 17, Jacqueline Wilson began contributing to the magazine that bore her name has become legend. Legends, however, are different from facts.

Across the Atlantic Ocean, Jacqueline ("Jackie") Kennedy was one of the most famous women in the United States. The widow of President John F. Kennedy, who was assassinated on November 22, 1963, she was celebrated for her youth and glamour during his presidency and her steadfast courage after his death. "Much of the shine of the Camelot legend emanated from Jackie Kennedy," *Newsmakers 1994* explained in her obituary. "Her stylishness in the White House was balanced with a historical sense of ceremony and dignity in preserving the young president in the nation's memory after his murder."[5]

In early 1964, when the magazine was launched, Jackie Kennedy was as well known and popular in Great Britain as British exports The Beatles were in the United States. Wilson admits the magazine was most likely not named after her. "I don't know whether or not I was meant to take Mr. Cuthbert or Mr. Tate's remark literally, but I did," she later confessed to the London *Guardian*. "However, I do believe that Mr. Gordon Small, the brilliant first editor of *Jackie*, has said that the name was a committee decision. 'Jackie' was a name of the times, because of Jackie Kennedy—every second hairdresser was called Jackie."[6]

GAINING EXPERIENCE

Although Jacky Wilson's passion was penning fiction, writing nonfiction articles gave her more than experience. It forged a deeper connection with other women her age; they opened up to the young reporter in ways they might not have if she had been older. That connection remained after Jacky grew up.

Today, Wilson admits her fictional accounts of girls enduring abusive homes and cruelty at school were inspired in part by the teens she met. Her novels remain deeply controversial, partly because she never shies away from describing the gritty reality of her character's lives, and partly because her fans usually begin reading them in elementary school. Yet the novelist has always refused to compromise. Her books are often dark, often disturbing. Why does she feel the need to write about such difficult issues?

The answer can be found not so much in her experiences as a reporter in Scotland, but in her childhood in Kingston-on-Thames, where she endured experiences radically different from the ones found in the stories then lining the shelves of the children's section.

Seen here, German air raid damage inflicted on Sheffield, England, on December 13, 1940, during the Second World War. Bomb craters in the main streets were a common sight throughout the war. Jacqueline Wilson's parents met during the war while both worked for the British Admiralty.

A Brief Time in Bath

LOOKING BACK, AUTHOR Jacqueline Wilson often recalls her childhood home as a sort of battlefield. She saw herself as the neutral country, caught between her parents' opposing armies. "I always said I wouldn't take sides because that's so horrible," she later told the London *Guardian*.[1] Yet it was an actual war—the Second World War—that brought her parents together.

World War II broke out in September 1939, pitting the Allied powers of Great Britain and France (and later the United States and the Soviet Union) against the Axis powers of Nazi Germany, Fascist Italy, and Imperial Japan. After the French were defeated in 1940, the Nazi war machine turned its attention on defeating Great Britain. The Nazis first sought to soften the island nation's defenses with bombing runs before an actual German invasion could take place.

For months, German forces unleashed an unrelenting air assault on Great Britain's military installations, peaking at some 1,500 missions a day. The Royal Air Force lay in ruins from these attacks, with most airfields and numerous planes destroyed. Then, late on the night of August 24, 1940, a handful of German Luftwaffe bombers went astray. Instead of hitting a military target, they unleashed their payload on a civilian target: London. The attack killed several unarmed civilians and destroyed a number of homes in the British capital. The British were outraged.

In response to the attacks, the country's prime minister, Winston Churchill, ordered the Royal Air Forces to respond in kind. The day after the attack, some 40 British bombers entered German airspace and dropped bombs over Berlin. Physical damage was minimal. The emotional damage on the German public, however, was far greater.

Despite invading more than half-a-dozen countries, Germany had remained relatively unscathed until the attack of August 7, 1940. The country's leader, Adolf Hitler, was furious. "When the British Air Force drops two or three or four thousand kilograms of bombs, then we will in one night drop 150-, 230-, 300-, or 400,000 kilograms," he pledged. ". . . we will raze their cities to the ground."[2]

Throughout September, the German air forces under Hitler's command did their best to make his pledge come true. For 57 consecutive days beginning on September 7, Luftwaffe bombers shifted their focus from military targets to civilian ones. The nightly blare of air raid sirens sent thousands of Londoners underground to shelter in subway tunnels and basements. There they endured crowded conditions with poor sanitation and little privacy. Above ground, incendiary bombs unleashed infernos that swept across the city. Hundreds were burned alive.

Such nightly attacks continued for the next eight months. German air raids spread across outlying cities, including Bath, Bristol, Manchester, and Liverpool. The Germans also dropped bombs on portions of Ireland and Scotland. By May 1941, nearly 40,000 British civilians, including approximately 5,000 children, had been killed. Wilson remembers her mother telling her about traveling up to London from her home in Kingston, "and she did say that it was always so strange because you would say goodbye to somebody after a day in London and yet never quite know if you were ever going to see them again."[3]

The focus on civilian targets also extracted an enormous toll from Hitler's seemingly indomitable war machine. Until then, his military had been undefeated and his dreams of world domination, as described in a popular book he wrote while locked in a Munich prison cell, seemed possible.

PATH TO WAR

Following its defeat in the First World War (1914–1918), Germany was economically devastated. After the war, Germany was required to compensate countries it had attacked, while at the same time it was forced to endure a reduction in its territory. The country suffered greatly during the 1920s. World War I veteran Adolf Hitler thought he knew why Germany was suffering. He believed the nation was betrayed by traitors and champions of democracy, as well as by minority groups, like German Jews, who according to him, stole all of Germany's wealth. Attempting to seize power in 1923, Hitler was imprisoned instead. He spent his jail term writing a book he called *Mein Kampf* (German for *My Struggle*).

"Although *Mein Kampf* was long, clumsily written, and poorly organized, it did serve to outline Hitler's fundamental ideas," explains *Historic World Leaders*. "Defining nature as a relentless struggle between superior and inferior species, and between strong and weak individuals within each species, the Nazi conception of the world saw racial struggle as a 'ubiquitous instinct for racial purity.'"[4]

The book described a reunited Germany and Austria ruled by Aryans: Hitler's super race of blue-eyed blonds. Campaigning after his release with the National Socialist German Worker's Party (or Nazi Party), Hitler blamed Jews for Germany's problems. He promised to lower prices and to increase employment. The message found millions of eager listeners.

In 1933, the Nazis won a majority in the Reichstag, the German parliament similar to the U.S. Congress. As a result of the elections, President Paul von Hindenburg appointed Hitler chancellor of Germany. After a suspicious fire leveled the Reichstag, Hitler, as head of the government, was granted emergency powers.

Soon after, Hitler restricted freedom of speech, the press, and assembly, while rendering the Nazis the only legal political party in Germany. Most notoriously, the Nazi government segregated people of Jewish origin in ghettos and relocated them to concentration camps. In less than a decade, Hitler's "Final Solution" would lead to the murder of millions of non-Aryans—not only Jews but also Catholics, the disabled, and numerous others. More than 6 million Jews alone would be killed.

In the years prior to World War II, Germany began rebuilding its air force and army, even as Britain's grew increasingly old and obsolete. Utilizing fast-moving infantry troops, armored tanks, and air support to crush opposition, Hitler's army trained in blitzkrieg, or "lightning war." In 1938, Germany annexed Austria and Czechoslovakia without a shot being fired. Many European powers did not protest. They wanted to appease Hitler, hoping to prevent another world war.

Following the Munich Conference in 1938, Prime Minister Neville Chamberlain of Great Britain assured his countrymen that the agreement signed between Britain and Germany was "symbolic of the desire of our two peoples never to go to war with one another again. . . . I believe it is 'peace for our time.'"[5]

The peace was not to last. On September 1, 1939, German armies invaded Poland. Two days later, Britain and France declared war against Germany. Just over two weeks later, German forces defeated the outgunned Polish army. In a single day—May 10, 1940—Hitler's lightning war crushed the opposing armies of Belgium, France, and Holland. Britain would now face Germany alone.

LOVE AMONG THE RUINS

Great Britain prepared for total war. As described on the Web site Britannia.com:

> Cities were blacked out, rationing was imposed and rigidly enforced; children from the larger cities were moved into the countryside, clouds of barrage balloons filled the English skies, housewives turned in their pots and pans for scrap, iron fences, railing and gateposts disappeared into blast furnaces, gas masks were issued to every single person, including babies; total blackout was imposed and rigorously enforced by air raid wardens. . . . British beaches were mined, protected by

barbed wire; tank traps and other obstacles to invading forces appeared everywhere; air raid shelters were dug in back gardens and London subway stations prepared for their influx of nightly sleepers.[6]

By focusing on civilian targets during their blitz, German forces offered England's Royal Air Force the opportunity to rebuild. In addition to planes and airstrips, the British constructed a more sophisticated tracking system that allowed them to follow the course of German fighters as soon as they took off from their bases in Europe.

British preparations for war involved nearly everyone in the country, soldier and civilian alike. "British industry mobilized every person not on military service into production," explains Britannia.com. "Even the old and retired were called on to play their part as plane spotters, air-raid wardens and night watchmen. But single women played a major role. They had to report immediately to work in war industries or to work on the nation's farms in the so-called Women's Land Army."[7]

As young men left the country to fight the Nazis, women often took over the jobs they once held. Jacqueline Wilson's mother, Margaret Clibbons, was barely out of her teens when she left her home in Kingston for Bath, nearly 100 miles (161 km) away. There she began working as a clerk for the Admiralty, which oversaw the Royal Navy. Also assigned to the Bath Admiralty was 23-year-old Harry Aitken, Wilson's father. His poor eyesight had kept him from being a soldier.

They both arrived in 1943. In Bath, Aitken worked on the design of a new submarine. Once a week, he left to go to an Admiralty-sponsored dance at the Pump Room. There he met Clibbons; the two danced and talked and made plans to see a movie together.

Watching the film *Now, Voyager*, Clibbons enjoyed the romantic efforts of its hero and often read novels like 1936's *Gone with the Wind*, which featured similarly dashing men and the women who loved them. Aitken, on the other hand, was practical and moody.

So what attracted Clibbons to Aitken? "It wasn't as if you had much choice," Clibbons later explained to her daughter. "There weren't many men around, they were all away fighting. I'd got to twenty-one and in those days you were starting to feel as if you were on the shelf if you weren't married by then. So, I decided your father would do."[8]

The couple wasted little time on courtship. "Because it was slightly bizarre times, I think they got engaged three months after meeting," Wilson explains. Only a few months after Aitken proposed with an emerald and diamond ring, they married.[9]

Relying on the help of a friend in Belfast, Ireland, Clibbons managed to get a long white lace dress and veil when wartime rationing meant most British brides had to make do with outfits using parachute silk. After the ceremony in Kingston's St. John's Church and a short Oxford honeymoon, they returned to Bath.

Life changed soon after. Margaret Aitken was pregnant.

PEARL HARBOR

By late 1941, Great Britain was no longer alone in its fight against Nazi Germany. The United States had entered the conflict following the Japanese attack on Pearl Harbor. Even before officially entering the war, the United States was a valuable ally to Great Britain through its Lend-Lease program, which supplied the United Kingdom and other Allied nations with war materiel.

On Sunday, December 7, 1941, Japanese forces launched a sneak attack against the U.S. Pacific Fleet based in Pearl

Harbor, Hawaii. Following the nearly two-hour bombing raid, some eight U.S. battleships were damaged with five sunk and more than 2,400 Americans killed. The next day, President Franklin Delano Roosevelt asked the U.S. Congress to declare war on Japan; Britain joined in this declaration. According to The History Place, after Japan's allies, Germany and Italy, declared war on America on December 11, "the European and Southeast Asian wars have now become a global conflict with the Axis powers; Japan, Germany and Italy, united against America, Britain, France, and their Allies."[10]

The American entry into the war altered the course of the conflict. Along with the Nazi defeat at Stalingrad, Russia, American forces won decisive victories in 1943. The invasion of continental Europe by more than 160,000 Allied forces during the D-Day landings at Normandy in France on June 6, 1944, sent Nazi forces into a slow and inexorable retreat. Less than a year later, Germany surrendered. Following two atomic bomb attacks on Hiroshima and Nagasaki, Japan, in the summer of 1945, the Japanese surrendered as well.

World War II was over. Europe—and much of the world—faced the incredible job of rebuilding. And in Bath, England, Jacqueline Aitken was born on December 17, 1945.

Money was already tight for Harry and Margaret Aitken. The addition of a child did not help. Writing in *My Secret Diary*, Jacqueline Wilson recalled her childhood: "There were a lot of arguments. Biddy [her mother] and me, Harry and me, Biddy and Harry against me—and most frequently of all, Biddy and Harry arguing between themselves."[11]

They fought regularly, their battles waged in the spaces they called home. The small family frequently moved,

As a child growing up in England in the years after World War II, Jacqueline Wilson endured considerable poverty. She grew up in a "council flat"—government-sponsored housing that was built just after the war.

living with the future author's grandparents or in furnished rooms. Jacky's nursery was the small rug in her parent's bedroom—"which can't have done much for their relationship either."[12]

In the United Kingdom, the job of reconstruction fell to an industrial-governmental partnership. Government employment skyrocketed. For a draftsman who had left school at 14, becoming a civil servant meant a guaranteed wage and a better life for Harry Aitken, as well as for his family.

THE COUNCIL FLAT

Harry Aitken added the family name to a long waiting list for "council flats," or government-sponsored housing, soon after Jacky's birth. She was six when they were finally able to move into an apartment in Cumberland House. The family was overjoyed.

"Nowadays, council estates are a slightly tougher place to live," admits Wilson, "and so that when I say with pride that I was brought up on a council estate, more gentile people in England raise their eyebrows, but it was actually quite a tame place. It was simply a place where you paid quite low rent and got for those times a reasonably good flat."[13]

Finding a home for the family in London was an enormous challenge. "Particularly just after the war, quite a lot of council flats were built simply because so many buildings had been damaged or just blown up by bombs," the novelist explains. "And so it was very very hard for young married couples to find anywhere and in those days it was very difficult if you had a baby to get rented accommodation anywhere."[14]

As she later wrote, their new apartment seemed luxurious. No longer would she have to share a room with her parents. Her own bedroom even had its own closet, one she quickly filled with outfits bought by her mother or knitted by her grandmother. And perhaps more important, the apartment was warm. "There was central heating!" she recalled in her memoir *Jacky Daydream*. "No more huddling over a smoking fire in the living room and freezing to death in the bedroom, having to dress under the eiderdown [a type of comforter] in the winter."[15]

Did you know...

While the Aitken family may not have had every modern convenience, they did enjoy one in particular. In June 1953, Jacky's parents purchased an 11-inch (28-centimeter) television. It received just one channel—the BBC—which broadcast in black-and-white. The family purchased the TV to watch Elizabeth II be crowned. Her coronation as the queen of England was the first such ceremony to be televised.

Young Jacky was unimpressed. Watching the brand-new television alongside her parents and grandparents, she later explained, "We all knew it was a momentous occasion. It was also very very very boring. . . . I sloped off to play with my paper dolls."

Her mother complained that she should be watching this once-in-a-lifetime event. "Biddy's telling-off was half-hearted. She was yawning and fidgeting herself."*

*Jacqueline Wilson, "The Coronation," *Jacky Daydream*. New York: Doubleday UK, 2007, p. 169.

For the first time, family members could enjoy a daily bath without having to haul hot water for a tin tub. Instead, the Aitkens now had an actual bathtub with hot and cold running water piped in. "It's just so extraordinary," Wilson admits, "I mean it shows that I've lived a long time, because it seems so very strange even to my ears . . . we didn't have a washing machine, we didn't have a telephone—just all the things that people take totally for granted—we didn't have a car until I was in my mid-teens. And yet I don't think we felt particularly deprived at all."[16]

Her mother's joy was tempered by one concern. She did not want her daughter educated with the other council children. Instead, Jacky was enrolled at Latchmere because her mother "didn't want me to go to school at the nearest school at Kingsnympton, the neighboring council estate," the writer explained. "She got it into her head that the Kingston school *furthest* from our flats was the best one, and somehow or other wrangled me a place there."[17]

It may have offered a superior education. It was also two miles (3.2 km) away. The Aitkens did not own a car. Jacky could not even ride a bike. Her mother tried to position her daughter on the back of her own bicycle, but Jacky was too cumbersome. She would have to walk to school. "It wasn't that unusual to let young children walk to school by themselves in those days," the writer later explained. "I liked my half hour's walk through the quiet suburban street. I'd make up stories inside my head or talk to imaginary friends."[18] Sometimes she would be unaware of the fact she was talking to herself until she noticed strange looks from passersby. "I already knew I was going to be a writer," she confessed. "Sometimes I'd pretend to be grown up and a famous author and I'd interview myself."[19]

Jacqueline Wilson's parents endured a loveless marriage because they grew up in an era when divorce was considered a taboo. As a result, she recalls them fighting often and violently.

The trip home was more challenging. She faced bullies from neighboring estates. Enduring a few fights was difficult, but it was nothing compared to what she faced in her own home.

BATTLES ON THE HOME FRONT

After moving to Kingston-on-Thames, young Jacky's life improved somewhat. Her father's rages did not. Writing in her book, *Jacky Daydream*, she described how divorce was taboo as a subject. Yet there were times she wished her parents would get divorced because as she put it, "there were so many screaming fights. . . . Sometimes I was caught up in a quarrel too, both of them yelling at me, appealing to me, while I begged not to have to take sides. Sometimes I simply listened from my bedroom while they argued endlessly, whipping each other with cruel words, then slapping and shoving, hating and hurting."[20]

Jacky had barely started school before her mother began working. It was unusual for a married woman with a child to work outside of the home in those days, but as Jacqueline Wilson recalled, "Biddy was very happy to go out to work. Harry only gave her a meager amount for housekeeping and she hated being dependent on him."[21]

Her mother worked part-time at a cake shop, and then as a playground attendant. When Jacky was eight, her mother began working full-time as a bookkeeper at a company called Prince Machines. The extra income never seemed enough. Their deprivations were hardly unique; many families in England suffered after the war. Still, for a child who later described herself as a "sad, shy, weedy little kid," the challenges were especially difficult.

Although in the 1940s families were often larger than they are today, Jacqueline remained an only child. Without siblings at home or many friends at school, she retreated into a fantasy world of imaginary friends, beasts lurking in the shadows, and magic tying the two together.

Books were another means of escaping from her troubled home life. Jacky was reading by the time her family had moved into their council flat. Unlike many writers who recall childhood homes brimming with books, such things would have been a luxury in the Aitken household. She usually received one or two books as presents on her birthday or Christmas. For the rest of the year, there was the library.

"My Dad was such a complex man. I could be very frightened of him," she later told the London *Guardian*. "But on the other hand, he could bring back books from the library that were really inspired choices. And he took me to the National Gallery [a large, publicly funded art gallery], say, or for walks in the country, so he tuned into all the things I liked to do."[22]

At 10, Jacky had read every book in the children's wing that she found interesting. Her mother won Jacky the privilege of being able to check out books from the adult section of the library. By then, Jacqueline Aitken was not just reading stories. She was also writing them.

THE BAD SEED

In many ways, fiction resembles lying. The writer creates a world that does not really exist by making up stories that are believable enough to keep readers interested. Unlike liars, authors generally do not craft stories to harm others or to get away with something. Still, most writers have stretched the truth in real life at one time or another.

The Bad Seed was a 1956 American movie about a seemingly perfect eight-year-old girl who is actually a devious killer. Controversial when it was released, the film was X-certificated in England. Only adults were allowed to see it. That did not deter Jacky. The actress playing the lead, Patty McCormack, inspired a bit of fan worship for Jacky. She begged her parents to take her to see it. They refused.

Soon after, Jacky's favorite teacher, Mr. Townsend, gave the class a writing assignment. "My Day Out" was supposed to describe a special day spent with their parents. Unfortunately, Jacky did not have many of those. Her mother might take her shopping, her father might take her to look at art, but the three rarely did things as a whole family. Whenever they did, small disagreements usually escalated into shouting matches between her mother and father, while Jacky retreated into her own private world.

Instead of remembering a real outing, she constructed one. It began with her family happily taking the train to London. They visited the biggest bookstore in the city, Foyles, on Charing Cross Road. Jacky wrote about her mother buying her Susan Coolidge's *What Katy Did at School* while her father gave her Noel Streatfeild's *Tennis Shoes*. After visiting London's largest bookstore, naturally the family went to the largest toy store. At Hamleys, Jackie received a tiny teapot "no bigger than my thumbnail for my doll's house."[23] The imaginary outing concluded with the trio watching the movie Jacky was forbidden to see.

Although she had never seen *The Bad Seed*, Jacky quoted liberally from her mother's descriptions. When the assignment was due, her classmates handed in essays of a page or so; Jacky's ran over half-a-dozen pages.

The night after handing it in, Jacky discussed the assignment with her mother. Biddy was upset that her daughter had not mentioned the Old Cottage Dolls she had bought her. "You didn't buy them with me on a day out—they were my Christmas present," Jacky explained.

"You could have juggled the facts a little to make a good story," her mother suggested. "You *love* your dolls. And they cost a fortune."

"Yes, well, I put a lot else," Jackie offered. "I said you gave me lots of treats—and we all went to *The Bad Seed* in the evening."

Her mother was flabbergasted. "You stupid idiot! What sort of mother will he think me, taking you to a film like that! Have you handed the composition in?"[24]

Jacky admitted that she had. Her mother demanded that she tell Mr. Townsend the truth. But she was nervous. Attending school in England more than 50 years ago was radically different than today. Corporal punishment was often employed against rule breakers in 1950s schools. "If you so much as sneezed during 'Happy and Glorious' ["God Save the Queen"] you could get the cane," she later wrote.[25] While girls were not smacked with the thin rod as often as boys, Jacky still worried. Almost as bad as being punished, she could not stand disappointing her favorite teacher.

Sitting in class early the next morning, Jacky could barely breathe. Mr. Townsend noticed; soon she was at his desk confessing. After telling him that she had made up the entire essay, his reaction surprised her. He was not shocked or angry. "Mr. Townsend, are you cross with me for telling lies?" she asked.

"I don't think you were really lying, Jacky. You were just making things up. There's a big difference. You've got a very vivid imagination."[26]

The worst day of her life was transformed into one of the best. "I took the deepest breath in all the world," she later wrote, asking, "'Do you think I might be able to write stories one day?'"

"I'm sure you will," her teacher replied. [27]

A few days later, one of his assignments gave her a chance to prove it.

MEET THE MAGGOTS

"I very much wanted to be a member of a large family," Jacqueline Wilson later admitted. "It was too intense when it was just Biddy and Harry and me."[28] Although Jacky could not alter the size of her family, in her stories she could create any sort of family she wished. As an author, she would construct dozens of different families, but Mr. Townsend gave her a start.

Not long after handing in her fictionalized excursion essay, "My Day Out," Jacky noticed the thick stack of green notebooks covering Mr. Townsend's desk. He told the class they were meant for a special project. Actually having so many notebooks reflected the project's significance since paper was still in short supply nearly a decade after the end of World War II.

The students could choose their own topic to write about. One wanted to write about astronomy, another about France. Several of the boys named different sports for their essay. Jacky did not want to share her idea with the class. Instead, she approached Mr. Townsend and quietly asked if she could write a novel. "I think that's a brilliant idea, Jacky," he told her.[29]

It would be a short novel, just 21 pages including the table of contents. Still, it had seven chapters and would be Jacky's first completed story. It reflected her love for certain books and her disdain for others. Inspired by the Ruggles in *The Family from One End Street*, she gave her characters a similar, humorous last name. She called them the Maggots.

Jacky found the stable, middle-class families populating most of the books she read boring and unrealistic. The father was often a doctor or a minister. Money never seemed to be much of a problem. Everyone got along.

In her story, the father, Alf Maggot, was a bus driver. Like her own family, money was a constant struggle for the Maggots. Unlike Jacky's mom, Daisy did not earn a living but worked full-time raising the seven Maggot children. The eldest, 15-year-old Marilyn was, according to the author, "dead keen on boys. And boys were dead keen on her too." Ten-year old Mandy was based on Jacky's favorite child actress, Mandy Miller, while 12-year-old Marlene was based on the author. "Her interest is books," young Jacky wrote, "You can't drag her out of them."[30]

Each chapter was devoted to a sibling, which also included nine-year-old twin boys, Marmaduke and Montague, as well as Melvyn, and the youngest, Marigold. "The Maggots was not a particularly startling or stylish story," Wilson now admits, "but I can nowadays claim, jokingly, that I wrote my first novel at the age of nine."[31]

That early fictional work was just the start. She continued to write by keeping a journal, crafting short stories, and imagining the life of a writer. "I didn't really believe I had a chance of seeing my stories in print," she admitted in *Jacky Daydream*. "It was a daydream, like some girls long to be actresses or rock stars or fashion models."[32]

Although a bright girl with an active imagination and a love of reading, Jacqueline Wilson would drop out of school at age 16 and find her place in the world as a writer.

Finding the Words

"I HATED SCHOOL," Jacqueline Wilson later wrote in her second autobiography, *My Secret Diary: Dating, Dancing, Dreams and Dilemmas*. "I didn't mind Latchmere, my primary school, but I couldn't bear my five years at Coombe County Secondary School for Girls."[1]

Attending the school had never been part of her plans. Her father had attended a technical school and hoped his daughter could attend a grammar school, which would prepare her for college instead of just a job. Both of Jacky's parents hoped she could get into her mother's alma mater, the Tiffin Girls' School. Jacky shared their dreams.

Kingston families with money had numerous options for their children's schooling. Poor- and lower-middle-class families like Jacky's had just one chance. Their children needed to pass the eleven plus exam.

Designed to provide a track for students following elementary school, the test was taken after the student turned 11 (thus its name). Examined in English proficiency, arithmetic, and general intelligence by solving word problems, the scores determined what type of school test takers would attend. Students could go into a technical school, which provided training for a trade, or a secondary modern school. Most parents and their children taking the exam were focused on getting scores that assured entrance into a grammar school like Tiffin Girls'.

As Wilson later explained, "SAT tests are like little pimples compared with the huge boil of the 1950s eleven plus." For students like Jacky, "the eleven plus was our one chance to get to a grammar school and stay on to do all the right exams and go into one of the professions."[2]

Tiffin Girls' was the only academically challenging school in the Kingston area that did not charge for students to attend. "If you failed the eleven plus," she recalled, "you went to a secondary modern school and left at fifteen and started work right away. You worked and therefore you stayed working class."[3]

Jackie awoke the day of the eleven plus exam with "one of those head-filled-with-fog colds, when you can't breath[e], you can't hear, you can't taste, you certainly can't think," she explained in her autobiography, *Jacky Daydream*. "I was boiling hot and yet I kept shivering, especially when I was sitting there at my desk, ready to open the exam booklet."[4] Jacky read the questions in her booklet over and over.

It did not help. She could not understand them. "I'd never felt so frightened in my life," she later admitted. "I didn't know the answer to a single problem."[5]

She muddled through the English portion, but the word problems in the intelligence test seemed even harder than the arithmetic—and "maths" as they are called in Britain—were never her strong suit. Afterward, she felt alone among her peers. She knew that they had all done much better than she had.

It was months before she learned the results. Finally, one day her teacher, Mr. Branson, stood before the class, the large envelope in his hand. He removed the results and skimmed through them. Later, Jacqueline Wilson would write about how he told them: "Well done, some of you. The rest of you should be thoroughly ashamed."[6]

There was no privacy. Their teacher read the results aloud. "I was Jacqueline Aitken, then," Wilson wrote, "the first child on the register." All of her classmates could hear as the teacher announced, "Jacky Aitken . . . you have *not* passed your eleven plus."[7]

Having learned her fate, she left at lunch and ran to her mother's job. Jacky was out of breath when she arrived. For a moment she waited, until her mother looked up from her work. Noticing her daughter, she smiled. She was certain Jackie had passed. Why else would she run two miles (3.2 km)? "No, no—I've *failed*," Jackie cried.

Her mother gave her a hug. "Never you mind," her mother consoled. "Did you get a second chance?"[8]

Jackie had forgotten. Students who nearly passed were able to retake the eleven plus. That summer she tried again. This time she passed. Tiffin Girls', however, did not accept students who had to retake the exam.

COOMBE GIRLS

Located a few miles from Jacky's Kingston-on-Thames home in New Malden, Surrey, Coombe County Secondary School for Girls had opened just a few years before her admittance. The school was also one of the first comprehensives, offering a diverse education for children with a wide range of abilities. It provided two teaching streams, either secondary modern or grammar—the highest level where Jackie was placed.

"This system didn't make allowances for girls like me," she later explained. "I'd been put in group one [the highest level academically] where I held my own in English and most of the arts subjects but I definitely belonged in group nine for maths [the lowest level]!" She imagined designing the class schedule was already "nightmare enough without trying to accommodate weird girls like me—very good in some subjects and an utter dunce in others."[9]

Since making her literary reputation, the author has returned numerous times to give an award or make a speech at the school. She is impressed with what she sees. The students seem kinder, the faculty more understanding. She feels it is far different than when she attended. "There were pointless rules, fierce regulations about uniform, a strict standard of behavior," she remembers. "You were expected to *conform*. I was never very good at that."[10]

DEAR DIARY

Writers of memoirs are sometimes accused of blending fact and fiction. Time and prejudice often alters memory, but in other instances authors willfully misrepresent their life stories. For example, author James Frey admitted on national television that he had made up large portions of his best-selling memoir, *A Million Little Pieces*, which had topped the *New York Times* nonfiction paperback best-seller list. Using experiences from one's own life, however, in a fictional work is a common method of dealing with the accuracy dilemma. Young-adult authors Lois Lowry and Katherine Paterson each utilized this technique in *Autumn Street* and *Jacob Have I Loved*, respectively.

As a teenager, Jacky Aitken dreamed of writing fiction. As a best-selling novelist, Jacqueline Wilson authored not one, but two memoirs totaling more than 600 pages. The first, *Jacky Daydream*, described how her parents met, the challenging circumstances they endured just after World War II, and her experiences in primary school (the equivalent of elementary school in the United States). The memoir ended shortly after she took the eleven plus exam.

That book drew on recollections, memories triggered by old photographs and conversations with her mother (who by then was an active antique seller in her late eighties). Researching her second autobiography, *My Secret Diary: Dating, Dancing, Dreams and Dilemmas*, was more straightforward. She mainly examined her teenage diaries, which she still had in her possession over four decades later. Jacky's journal writing did not begin in earnest until she reached her teens. It was then that she was inspired by another young girl who kept a diary, Anne Frank.

Frank was a Jewish girl whose family fled Frankfurt, Germany, for Amsterdam, Holland, following Hitler's rise to power in 1933. After the Nazis invaded Holland in May 1940, they enacted anti-Jewish laws and began deporting thousands of Jews to the Auschwitz extermination camp. When Anne's older sister Margot received a letter of deportation, their father, Otto, was well prepared.

The managing director of a local food company, Otto Frank had constructed two hidden apartments within its

Anne Frank sits at her desk where she began her now-famous diary before going into hiding from the Nazis. Anne Frank's writing, published after World War II as The Diary of a Young Girl, *would inspire many young authors, including Jacqueline Wilson.*

warehouse. From June 1942 until August 1944, Anne shared the cramped quarters with her father, mother, and sister, along with the van Daan family (a father, mother, and their teenage son, Peter) and an elderly Jewish dentist.

During her time there, Anne kept a diary. "The diary was forcefully written and tells the story of the living together of the eight persons," explains the *Encyclopedia of World Biography*, adding, "This was often done in a humorous way, displaying considerable talent of observation, originality, and description. Anne was well able to convey to the reader the fears about discovery and the hopes about an end to the war."[11]

Anne also described her quarrels with her mother and a growing attraction to Peter. The group was discovered in 1944 and deported to different concentration camps. Only Otto survived. Anne died of typhus in the Nazi concentration camp Bergen-Belsen in March 1945, just weeks before it was liberated.

After the war, Otto discovered his daughter's diaries and had them published. "The cheerfulness of Anne's writing in such dangerous circumstances," explains the *Encyclopedia of World Biography*, "as well as her sensitivity and talent to describe difficult circumstances and the tragedy of her short life, made [Anne Frank's *The Diary of a Young Girl*] an instant success. The book was translated into over 30 languages, and a pocket book edition in Germany alone sold 900,000 copies, while several million copies of a United States publication of the diary were sold."[12]

Jacky read *The Diary of a Young Girl* over and over, until she could quote entire sections from memory. "I especially loved the parts where Anne says she wants to be a writer when she grows up," Jacqueline Wilson wrote in the first page of *My Secret Diary*. "I identified so strongly with that longing. I ached for Anne because she never had a chance to fulfill her huge potential."[13]

Compared to such a powerful work, the recollections of a teenage girl coming of age in 1950s Britain seemed to pale by comparison. Indeed, noting her teenage self's way of describing how she spent her time, Wilson commented, "My writing was certainly as limp as a lettuce in those days."[14]

WRITING DREAMS

As a teen, Jacky began to consider what it meant to be a writer. Her New Year's resolutions for 1960 mirrored other years. Sick of the permanents that left her hair frizzy, Jacky wanted long, straight hair. She wanted a boyfriend. And she wanted to write a book. "I'd *written* so-called books, heaps of them," she admitted in *My Secret Diary*, "but they were twenty-page hand-written efforts in Woolsworths notebooks. Most petered out halfway though. Some only progressed for a page or two."[15]

Jacky entered competitions, like 1960's *Daily Mirror* Children's Literary Competition. Although she did not win the newspaper's contest, she did earn a note informing her that her story had "reached the final stages of selection."[16] Like many aspiring professionals, she started to read books filled with information about her dream job—books about becoming a writer. She was soon disappointed with what she read. Most suggested that realism was not what children were looking for as readers.

Author Kathleen Betterton advised that "the writer for children must not attempt subtlety of character in which good and evil are blended."[17] Betterton believed children liked fantasy stories and hated anything too realistic. Jacky decided she was just abnormal; she wanted the stories she read to have more in common with the life she knew. Edith Blyton wrote some of the first books Jacky read as a child, but Blyton's autobiography left her cold. Jacky wondered how Blyton could "write all day, yet leave out everything about real life." "Her families don't quarrel," she complained in her diary, "her parents don't nag, her teenagers aren't interested in lipstick and boys, her children never listen to dirty stories or wet themselves, and she ignores babies and pregnancy and sex. Surely all these things must have some part in her life."[18]

Jacky wanted to write stories that reflected the life she knew. If she could not write those types of stories for children or teens, then she would write strictly for adults.

EARLY EFFORTS

All beginning writers must find their own voices—those unique styles that set them apart. And if they are successful, they find them. Regular readers of authors with a distinctive voice can identify their work even without seeing their name on the jacket. For Jacky, like all writers, developing

> ### Did you know...
>
> Besides books on writing, Jacky read widely. Among the books she mentions in her autobiographies are Margaret Mitchell's *Gone with the Wind*; Dodie Smith's *I Capture the Castle*; Richard Mason's *The World of Suzie Wong*; Frances Hodgson Burnett's *The Secret Garden* and *A Little Princess*; Charlotte Brontë's *Jane Eyre*; Grace Metalious's *Peyton Place*; and Keith Waterhouse's *Billy Liar*.

her talent meant writing hundreds of thousands of words no one ever read, novels she never finished, and stories that were never published.

Unlike her diaries, most of her early fiction has disappeared. Some were discarded by Jacky who was "ashamed because they were so childish, so awkward, so derivative," or thrown away by Biddy during her annual spring-cleaning. Jacky learned, however, that the best way to preserve her work was to jot it in a school notebook. Thinking the books contained work for school, her mother never threw those away.[19]

Because of such a notebook, Wilson was able to provide an excerpt of a story she wrote at 14 in one of her autobiographies. A romance, *The Story of Latina* suffered from the author's tendency to write lists in her fiction just as she did in her journals. "Her eyes gazed into his," she wrote, "a soft, intelligent bright blue which reminded him very much of the sea for although they were now calm and peaceful they had tints of violet, green, grey and black which showed they could change color in accordance to her mood."[20]

Latina was initially the same age as her creator, but as Wilson explained in *My Secret Diary*, "I clearly intended her to have a full-blooded romance with my hero so I added another three years to make it more respectable."[21] Latina's love interest was named Alan, after Jacky's primary school boyfriend.

And, just as her diary detailed what she wore, where she went, and who she encountered, the character of Alan suffered similar lists. "A knife in a sheath was fixed to his belt," she wrote, "a comb, handkerchief, map, wallet and some chocolate went into his trouser pockets and his windcheater pockets were filled with a packet of sandwiches, and two bottles, one containing brandy and one of plain water."[22]

In *The Story of Latina*, people are enduring a bizarre pandemic—an infectious disease that causes victims to grow an extra part of their body. The infected might grow an extra arm, leg, or head; Alan had grown an extra finger. The police were rounding up those who had the illness and sending men to one island, women to another "because a man and a woman might fall in love and have children who would naturally be disformed."[23]

The concept seemed radical for a novice storyteller, but was lifted heavily from something she had read. Today, Jacqueline Wilson admits to cribbing the entire scenario from a science fiction book she had read and loved—John Wyndham's *The Chrysalids*. In the 1955 novel, characters are exiled after growing extra fingers or other body parts.

While struggling with her own stories, Jacky labored over assigned essays. She generally enjoyed them, but in her diary she complained about a writing assignment given by Miss Pierce that she found childish. "Oh how I long to get a book published," Jacky wrote, "just to show Miss P. I have one in mind at the moment, a rather sordid story about teenagers. I long to shock Miss P. and show her that her quiet shy Jacky isn't what she thinks she is."[24]

Jacky's diary contained little information about the stories she was working on. Although 40 years later Wilson wished for more information because she remembered so little about those early efforts, she admitted in *My Secret Diary*, "I'm interested that I don't want to go into details . . . in my diary. I feel exactly the same way now. If I get a good idea, it's fatal to talk about it and even writing too many notes can destroy it."[25]

Like many novice writers, Jacky struggled to finish a project. Long descriptive lists of her character's physical traits or what they wore filled pages, but they did not maintain her interest. Still, she was learning by reading, not just what she liked but what she did not. Just as she rarely wrote "The End," in her own stories, she rarely read "The End" in books she considered boring: "I cannot bear persevering with a book when I don't like it."[26]

While crafting derivative science fiction tales, real-life drama was occurring all around her. Her diary might contain the odd entry about her parents' escalating arguments but her fiction did not yet draw upon her life. She wondered if her parents would divorce (which was quite rare 40 or 50 years ago). And by the summer of 1960, she realized that her mother was having an affair.

A SUMMER ROMANCE

While preparing for vacation, Jacky admired her mother's talent for packing a suitcase. As she looked over the artful arrangements of her clothes, she realized, however, that some things were missing. "What about my stuff?" she remembered asking. "My journals and my notebook and my black folder and–"

"You're not going to be huddled in a corner writing all day long," her mother told her. "You're on *holiday*."[27]

To Jacky, journaling, writing in her notebooks, reading her favorite novels—doing those things *was* a holiday. They provided an important escape from temperamental parents. The family's two-week sojourn looked bleak, until her mother left to pack her father's suitcase. Jacky managed to slip into her own luggage not just a diary and a notebook, but several books as well.

"Biddy sniffed when she saw me clutching [the novel] *Billy Liar* the next morning and Harry cursed when he picked up my suitcase (*Gone with the Wind* alone was like a couple of bricks), but I couldn't bear the thought of running out of reading material," Wilson remembered. "I had two long weeks sitting on a bench with four adults who would be talking amongst themselves. It's a wonder I didn't try to stuff our collected hardback edition of Jane Austen into my suitcase too."[28]

The family was spending the week in St. Ives and another in Newquay, both of which were beach towns several hundred miles from home. Accompanying them would be the adults Jacky called Uncle Ron and Aunty Grace. She was not related to them. "Biddy worked with Ron at Prince Machines and they were very close," Wilson explained in *My Secret Diary*. "I'm sure they'd have loved to go off on holiday, just the two of them. It seemed so strange for us all to go in this awkward fivesome. Why didn't Harry or Grace object?"[29]

Jacky felt bitter toward her often cold and distant father. "How happy we'd all be if Uncle Ron and Mum married," she wrote in her diary. "Dad would have Aunty Grace! (Two awkward ones together.) I am writing a lot of nasty things about him, we haven't had a quarrel or anything but I'm just fed up and truthfully admitting things I've loyally tried to ignore."[30]

Even as her diary writing took on the honest edge that would later distinguish her fiction, Jacky came close to achieving another goal she had set for herself. She was about to meet a boy.

In Newquay, she was up at first light. Downstairs in the hotel, she met Colin—a boy younger than she was, who, after a few games of table tennis, asked Jacky if she wanted to be his girlfriend. She refused. Undisturbed, he asked if she would prefer to be his friend Cookie's girlfriend. As she had not met him and was a bit put off by the oddness of his name, she said she did not want to be his girlfriend, either.

Then they met. As author Wilson later wrote, Cookie was "a boy with intense brown eyes, fair curly hair and a smooth golden tan."[31] While it might not have been love at first sight, it came awfully close. She and Cookie and Colin spent every spare moment together, until the hotel held a dance near the end of her parents' vacation. There she danced with Cookie, and they managed to get away from the hotel. Walking with him on the beach, Wilson remembered, "It was so dark I couldn't see anything at all. I had to cling to Cookie and he clung to me, and then we were kissing and whispering and wishing we could stay there forever."[32]

Although Jacky exchanged a few letters with Cookie after the vacation, the correspondence soon petered out. His mother even wrote to Jacky, apologizing because her son was "not very good at writing letters."[33] The brief summer romance meant Cookie never really became a proper boyfriend. But he would play a role in her development as an author as she began writing more stories that had their foundation in the events of her life.

While the lost romance hurt, in February of 1961 she admitted to her diary, "Ever since last summer I've been trying to write a novel. . . . I was convinced that I was writing what was to become a great classic, and dabbled around with it at the weekends and in the evenings." However, she soon decided that "it was only very adolescent escapism. I had no boyfriend or anything, and in the Summer I had spent a nice week with Cookie, so

I unconsciously comforted myself by my very infantile book about my 'adult' experience."[34]

Years later, Wilson regretted that she was hard on herself. She also wished she had kept the story. Two months after that entry, she confessed to her diary, "I'm going to write a book, but not yet, because 15 is too young, too immature. . . . I know I'm just a silly little fool, probably with absolutely no gift for writing at all, yet that doesn't prevent me from trying. I've got to be a writer and nothing else."[35]

DROPPING OUT

"I hated the whole *atmosphere* of school," she later wrote in *My Secret Diary.* "My heart would sink as I trudged up the path and went through the glass doors into the cloakrooms. There was always a fug of damp gabardines and old shoes as soon as you walked in. As the day progressed, the smells got worse."[36]

It was not just the outside atmosphere that Jacky found oppressive. It was the idea of conforming that wore her down. As an aspiring writer, she had little interest in society's expectations. Then again, society itself was changing. The 1960s was a time of generational upheaval, when ideas about family, work, gender, and race radically shifted. Across the Atlantic Ocean, protests against the U.S. involvement in Vietnam along with marches for civil and women's rights had, by the middle of the decade, transformed the country. Opportunities for many increased while attitudes toward work and family began to alter.

Although England underwent similar transformations, for Jacky Aitken, the choice to pursue uncertain freedom over a stable education had less to do with changing society than her own internal struggles. By the time she was 16, she believed that what she was learning at school paled in comparison to what she could learn on her own. And her work ethic was strong; she had even completed her first full-length novel, although she later admitted it "didn't even go so far as to have a title. It was some kind of teenagery book about two sisters who went on holiday together. I didn't have a sister and we didn't go on many exotic holidays, but there you go."[37]

By then, "My mom and dad didn't think there was any point in my staying on at school," she remembered.[38] Besides, Jacky knew what she wanted to do with her life. She wanted to be an author. She did not have any contacts or even an idea of how to get published. Despite the obstacles, she dropped out of Coombe's. Initially she was not a writer at all. She was a secretary.

The London offices of the Dundee publishing firm D.C. Thomson at 185 Fleet Street. Working at Thomson as a teenager would launch Jacqueline Wilson's career as a writer.

4

Magazine Work

DROPPING OUT OF high school is never a good idea. Lacking an education often means accepting low pay and few opportunities for advancement.

Jacqueline Aitken was more fortunate. After leaving Coombe County Secondary School for Girls at 16, she began attending a technical school. Over the course of a year's study, she would learn shorthand (a form of note taking that relied on symbols as substitutes for words) and typing so she could work as a secretary. Although it was hardly her dream opportunity, it was leavened because she shared the experience with her best friend, Christine.

Jacky had met Chris on their first day at the Coombe School for Girls. She immediately noticed the "smallish girl with long light-brown hair neatly tied in two plaits" sitting behind her in homeroom. Learning her name was Christine, she later wrote "I was pre-disposed to like girls called Christine." It had been the name of her best friend at primary school, and she "started to take proper notice of her."[1]

Teaming up to find their first class—an elusive art course—they discovered it was taught not in the main building but in a smaller one near the playground. Pushing their desks together in math class, they struggled with a subject in which they had little ability and even less interest. They dreamed of someday owning homes side by side just like their desks. "We don't live next door to each other now," Wilson explains, "but we did stay great friends all through school and went on to technical college together." Long into adulthood, they remained in touch.[2]

Having a friend helped, but Jacky desperately wanted to be a writer, not a secretary. Secretarial work was for her a fall-back position, something to pay the bills. Nearly five decades later, as a professional writer, she still dislikes being cooped up in an office. While some authors work at a schedule not terribly different from office workers, in her memoir *Jacky Daydream*, she explains, "I don't sit at my desk and write all day though—I'd find that incredibly boring and exhausting."[3]

During her time at the school, she was also in the midst of her first serious relationship. Her boyfriend, Peter, was a hairdresser. Pictures taken of Jacky at the time show a petite teenager overwhelmed by enormous hairdos. "It looked as if my life was all mapped out," she later concedes. Her mother "thought I should get a job as a secretary. I didn't want to be a secretary. I didn't want to settle down and marry Peter. I wanted to be a writer and lead a glamorous arty life in a picturesque book-filled garret. But it all seemed like a little girl day dream."[4]

At 17, Jacky began her first job as a junior secretary for J.M. Dent and Sons. The company had achieved success as the publisher of The Everyman's Library, a 1,000-book series of classics. Reporting for work her first day, Jacky noticed the books lining the shelves right near her desk. She recalled, "I do remember . . . looking up at the Jane Austen's and thinking this is my opportunity, I can read my way *all* around the book shelves. Needless to say, I didn't. I read the Jane Austens and the Bronte sisters, and I might have got as far as Dickens but that was that."[5]

Although not her dream job, the position had its advantages. As Wilson remembers, "the main secretary was often closeted in with the boss taking dictation or whatever, and so I did have a lot of time to spare by myself and I always loved reading so this seemed a good opportunity."[6]

HELP WANTED

The secretarial job, however, was short-lived. One day while reading the evening paper, she came across an advertisement that could have been written with her in mind. "Wanted! Teenage Writers!" it proclaimed. "I was a teenager," she remembered, "and I desperately wanted to be a writer, so I wrote off for further information."[7]

The advertisement was for a publisher, D.C. Thomson of Dundee, Scotland. Established in 1905, the company published everything from comic books to newspapers and was then in the midst of developing a magazine for teenagers. Unlike many similar publications, however, it hoped to employ teens to contribute much of the content. It was a perfect opportunity.

Jacky quickly responded to the ad, receiving back a set of writer's guidelines from D.C. Thomson. She studied these carefully, and then submitted a humorous article. "To my astonishment they wrote back saying they wanted to publish my piece and would pay me three guineas." In U.S. currency the amount was about five dollars. In her book *Jacky Daydream*, Wilson admits, "Even in those long ago days in the 1960s, three guineas wasn't a lot of money, but it meant the world to me. Someone actually liked my writing and wanted to buy my article and publish it."[8]

Although magazine or newspaper staff writers often generate some of their own ideas, their employers suggest many other ideas; freelance writers like Jacky usually come up with the bulk of their stories on their own. For Jacky, generating those ideas, writing articles, and submitting them for publication—all while working full-time as a secretary—was quite demanding. Still, she took to the discipline quickly, submitting a new article nearly every day. Despite her productivity, she was not ready to quit her day job.

A month later all that changed. D.C. Thomson wanted to hire her as a full-time staff writer. There was only one

Did you know...

In 2010, Jacqueline Wilson's old publisher, D.C. Thomson, began publishing the *Official Jacqueline Wilson Magazine*. According to its Web site, it is "a magazine for girls aged 7–12 who love reading. Based on best-selling author, Jacqueline Wilson, her books and characters."

problem. The job was in Scotland, more than 200 miles (321.8 km) away.

A MAGAZINE NAMED *JACKIE*

Leaving home for the first time is usually a bit traumatic for almost any young person. Some children leave for extended stays at summer camp, others attend boarding school. For most, college is the first lengthy period away from home. Instead of going to college, Jacqueline Aitken was going to work.

Quitting a tedious job and abandoning an unpleasant home life seemed ideal to Jacky. Arriving in Scotland, however, she soon battled homesickness. Sometimes she even went into the local Woolworth's department store because it was identical to the one at home.

Young, single women in the 1960s occupied a gray area between childhood and adulthood. Jacky's mother worried about her being off on her own. Like many young unmarried women then, Jacky could not live in an apartment. Instead, she moved into a hostel. Similar to the low-cost hotels popular with backpackers and budget vacationers today, the Church of Scotland Girls' Hostel offered shared bedrooms and some of the amenities of home, like a kitchen and a living area. Unlike hostels today, however, the Girls' Hostel Jacky was moving into had strict rules enforced by a matron—an older woman who acted like a combination parent/landlord.

"The matron didn't want to take me at first," Jacky recalled, "as all her rooms were full, but she saw I was quite small and squeezed a put-u-up bed into the linen cupboard and turned it into a weeny bedroom for me."[9] The arrangement made the newcomer popular with the other girls during the chilly winter.

An older building, the hostel lacked central heating and the rooms got quite cold. Jacky's tiny room, however, had hot pipes for the clothes, which kept her space quite toasty. "All the girls wanted to be my friend so they could squeeze into my room with me," she wrote in the epilogue to *Jacky Daydream*. "We used to squash up together, giggling in the dark, having midnight feasts."[10]

Back home, life changed drastically for her parents. She recalled:

> It's strange, because most people would use [the council flat] as a base and save up and then maybe after about five years they would get a mortgage and a house and move out. But my parents, I think never felt totally united and didn't really work together to do this. . . . After I moved out at seventeen, my mother stayed around for a while and then I think she inherited my grandparent's house and then sold that and got her own place, but my father lived on in Cumberland House slightly bizarrely until he died when he was in his fifties.[11]

Her new job had its own challenges. The planned magazine was not yet ready, but Jacky kept quite busy. Back home she had written numerous nonfiction articles "about the 'so-called joys' of being a teenager," but the company also "had lots of story magazines so I wrote a lot of fiction for them too. And then when I went actually up to Scotland to work for them, I wrote reader's letters, I wrote horoscope columns, I wrote anything they asked."[12] Looking back, Wilson admits:

> D.C. Thomson is a slightly strange firm, it's very paternalistic—or it certainly was in those days—but it was a wonderful opportunity because the staff on each magazine was quite small and so everybody was given a chance to do more or less

everything and because the printers were all part of the firm, I mean you physically took your copy up to the printers and then saw it in the magazine almost straight away.[13]

For a few months, Jacky was contributing to magazines aimed at adult women like the weekly *Red Letter* magazine and the monthly *Annabelle*. Although she was looking forward to writing pieces for teenagers, just being able to write as a full-time job was a heady experience. "It was very good for my confidence, and as a way of making different friends," she explained to journalist Amanda Craig. "I was very poor—I had £2.15 left after rent. . . . But I knew that I didn't want to be a typist."[14]

While working as a writer for the women's magazines, Jacky met once a week with her editors, Mr. Tate and Mr. Cuthbert. During one such meeting they told her the teen magazine she would be writing for would be launched in early 1964. It would be called *Jackie*.

A number of sources, including the author's own Web site, claim the magazine was named after one of D.C. Thomson's youngest journalists. The truth is a bit more nuanced. In 2007, a documentary titled *Jackie Magazine: A Girl's Best Friend* looked at the publication's history. Its first editor, Gordon Small, said the name was a committee decision and that Jackie was the name of the times. Jacky Aitken probably influenced the choice (and having a writer named Jacky writing for the magazine *Jackie* was a nice bit of symmetry) but so did Jackie Kennedy and the many young women with the name in the early 1960s.

Whatever it was named, *Jackie* was an immediate success. For the first year of its publication, it averaged monthly sales of 350,000. By the end of the decade, that number would reach nearly half-a-million copies, exclusively in Great Britain. "Whenever I'm giving talks to

Jackie *was an immediate success as a magazine for teenage girls when it first began publication in the early 1960s. In the 1970s, it published a mix of fashion stories, beauty tips, gossip, short stories, and comic strips. Seen here, a comic strip love story called* Dear Diary, *published in 1975.*

families it's always a great one to bring up because the mothers in the audience," Wilson explains, "whenever I mention the name . . . they immediately nudge each other and go, 'Oh my, God, I remember reading *Jackie* magazine.'"[15]

Like teen magazines today, *Jackie* was trendy, offering tips on hairstyles and fashion. In fact, Jacky not only wrote for the magazine bearing her name, she also modeled for it. "I was not a particularly gorgeous or stylish teenager," she admits, "but sometimes I stood in for the latest fashion, and there was an article about getting engaged and they used my hand for that. When you were a journalist at DC Thomson, you had to be willing to do everything."[16]

"*Jackie* was considered a bit outrageous in its day," she later told the *Guardian*, "but if we could have seen some of the articles in teenage magazines now, we would have been amazed."[17]

Besides promoting young male pop music and movie stars, the publication influenced the tastes and values of its audience. As one academic study of the magazine pointed out, "In *Jackie* D.C. Thomson is not merely, 'giving girls what they want . . .' A concerted effort is never the less made to win and shape the consent of the readers to a particular set of values."[18] The study also asserted that publications for men usually focus on leisure pursuits and hobbies—from fitness to motorcycles—with "no consistent attempt to link interests with age. . . . Instead there are a variety of options available, many of which involve participation outside the home."[19]

Women's magazines are different. Those publications focus on their reader's age, assigning certain goals depending on the average age of their readership. "[*Jackie*] is ascribing to age certain ideological meanings," the study explained. "Adolescence comes to be synonymous with

Jackie's definition of it." Reading articles in the magazine gave the impression that "all girls want to know how to catch a boy, lose weight, look their best and be able to cook."[20]

By 1965, after having authored more than 60 articles, Jacky had her own issues with *Jackie*. "I was thrilled to see my stories in print (though the magazine editors cut out my finest descriptive passages and pared each character down to a sad stereotype)," she recalled, "but it wasn't the sort of fiction I really wanted to write. I wasn't interested in the glossy fantasy world of the magazines. I wanted to write about young people and their problems but I didn't want to pretend there were the easy solutions offered up in the magazine stories."[21]

At 19, she was ready for new opportunities. She wanted to be a novelist. During her time as a journalist, she had completed several novels. Unfortunately, she was unable to get them published. By then, however, Jacky had other things to occupy her mind. She had fallen in love.

Jacqueline Wilson first got her start as an author of adult crime novels—a genre with a long and storied history. One of the most famous crime novelists was Dashiell Hammett, author of the 1930 crime classic The Maltese Falcon. Seen here, the cast of the 1941 film version of that novel, from left, Humphrey Bogart, Peter Lorre, Mary Astor, and Sidney Greenstreet.

Criminal Decisions

THE LOVE BLOOMED at work. William Millar Wilson was a printer at D.C. Thomson when he met the teenage journalist. The courtship was fairly brief; on August 28, 1965, Jacqueline Aitken and Wilson were married. "I was nineteen!" Jacqueline Wilson offered with some astonishment in an interview. A photo appearing in her memoir *Jacky Daydream* shows the well-dressed couple on their wedding day. She looked like exactly what she was—a young woman barely out of high school.[1]

The couple moved to London. Her husband was unable to find work because his former employer had been a nonunion firm. As a result, union-run printers in the city would not hire him. "He had always been a kind of active, outdoors sort of person," Wilson explained, "and so he thought that he might like a career as a policeman. So he applied and was taken on by the Metropolitan Police Service, which was the London Police, and very much enjoyed it and he became a career policeman from then on."[2]

Jacqueline Wilson was done working for *Jackie*. She was not, however, done writing. She recalled: "I did carry on writing for many teenage magazines and also women's magazines. I continued writing for these magazines, mostly anonymously, for many years because they paid very good money. . . . So it was a wonderful supplement to the money coming into the house. I got used to writing at least 10,000 words of magazine fiction a week. . . . I really did work hard then."[3] What kinds of stories was she writing then? "I wrote sort of mildly romantic short stories," Wilson explains, describing the bulk of her work in her early twenties, "and even wrote, we had 'confession magazines,' and these were even better because they were totally anonymous and paid the best of all. I didn't like to write these stories but certainly I did like it when we didn't have any money worries."[4]

In 1967, when Wilson was 21, her daughter Emma Fiona was born on February 16. She did not want her daughter to be the third generation of only daughters. She dreamed of having half-a-dozen children who happily played in the kitchen as she prepared dinner. As she told one newspaper, "For the first few months of [Emma's] life she didn't sleep more than two hours, ever, at a time." Her husband "made it pretty plain that if I wanted any more I'd be coping on my own. And I did want some more, but never quite absolutely enough to make sure they arrived."[5]

By the time Emma was a toddler, Wilson had embarked on a larger project. It would incorporate all she had learned of police investigations through her husband, along with the messy, real-life families she had dreamed of describing as a teenager. She would become a crime novelist.

THE BUSINESS OF CRIME

By her early twenties, Jacqueline Wilson was ready to make good on her oft-repeated New Year's pledge to become a novelist. After penning a book about two sisters on vacation, Wilson remembered:

> In my late teens, I wrote about three more novels. One of them was a children's book, and I did send that to my ex boss at J.M. Dent to see what he thought of it. And I remember vividly, he wrote back a very kind letter saying sensibly that he didn't think it quite was working but saying nice things about my characterization, etc. And I was such a fool, I thought this meant he was just sorry for me and just being nice and didn't realize that if you get an actual thick two page letter from the publisher it does mean they are actually quite interested in you.[6]

Other than having a novel that had come in third in a contest sponsored by the Society for Women Writers and Journalists, Wilson had little luck getting published. "My first few novels all got turned down," she admitted to EssentialWriters.com, adding, "It's horrible—but you just take it on the chin."[7]

Wilson's first published book came about because of her daughter. Just as her mother had done with her, Wilson spent time at the Kingston Children's Library selecting reading material for Emma. "I found a series edited by Leila Berg," Wilson explained to the *School Library Journal.*

"She thought that for a child in a bleak housing estate, the world pictured in reading books, where everybody lived in pretty houses with manicured lawns would be hard for those kids to relate to, so she started a series of books called Nippers."[8]

Wilson did not realize that Berg approached the authors; they did not approach her. Writing a book on speculation—without a contract—was a risky approach, but in this case Wilson's ignorance worked in her favor. "I counted up the number of words on each page," she remembered, "saw that there were 32 pages, and so had a go, and sent *Richard's Birthday* off to Leila Berg, and, wonderfully for me, she bought it."[9]

Ricky's Birthday was published in 1973. By then, she had placed her first full-length novel. "I wrote it with enormous speed, because I had a young daughter then and my

Did you know...

After regularly entering contests as a young writer, Jacqueline Wilson decided to sponsor one of her own. She invited her readers to contribute a chapter to 2002's *The Worry Web Site*. The novel about a teacher-designed site for students to write about their problems began online in 2001. Some 15,000 entered the contest and "it was agonizing only to be able to choose one," Wilson wrote. "But that one story was so special that it simply had to be the winner. It's by Lauren Roberts, age twelve."*

* Jacqueline Wilson, "Lisa's Worry," *The Worry Web Site*. New York: Yearling, 2005, p. 82.

then husband had a fortnight [two weeks] off work and we couldn't afford to go anywhere," Wilson remembered. "So we did a trade off and he looked after my daughter and I wrote the novel in a fortnight which now, makes me quite weak at the very thought, but I worked all day long and well into the night I was so desperate to get it done . . . and then I can't remember if that one went out to several publishers, but certainly I sent it to Macmillan."[10]

The publishers of *Ricky's Birthday* decided they would also publish Wilson's first adult novel, *Hide and Seek*. Then they surprised her by explaining that they would bring it out on "their crime list, which was weird to me because I hadn't thought of it as a crime novel at all." Wilson said books in that genre were "about the only sort of book I didn't enjoy reading, but because Macmillan was happy to publish me, I was happy to go along with it."[11]

A HISTORY OF CRIME NOVELS

By the time Wilson was writing in the 1970s, crime novels had been successful for decades. In the 1930s and 1940s, the novels of Raymond Chandler, Dashiell Hammett, and Mickey Spillane featured flawed detectives and femme fatales—the charming women who led them into danger. The novels these men wrote proved so popular that they were adapted into films, which are today collectively known as a popular subgenre of movies, film noir. With their dark streets, fog-shrouded alleys, and damaged main characters, both the novels and film noir offered audiences a new type of leading man, the antihero. Unlike traditional heroes with noble values and virtues, the antihero is more self-interested and flawed. Some were addicts, others former criminals, yet ultimately they often succeeded where traditional heroes failed.

One thing that made these novels popular at the time, especially Chandler's *The Big Sleep*, Hammett's *The Maltese Falcon*, and Spillane's *I the Jury*, was their heightened violence and risqué content. Dismissed as trash at the time of their initial publication, the literary merits of these books, particularly Chandler's and Hammett's work, are widely recognized today.

In 1954, Evan Hunter had his first success with *The Blackboard Jungle*, a gritty novel that was adapted into a film the following year. Besides working as a screenwriter (penning, for example, *The Birds* for director Alfred Hitchcock) he gained tremendous success under the pen name Ed McBain as an author of police procedurals.

As recounted in *Authors and Artists for Young Adults*, the novelist remembered "When I was beginning to write, I wrote a great many detective stories for the pulp magazines. I wrote not only police stories, but private eye and man-on-the-run and woman-in-jeopardy, the whole gamut." Two years after *The Blackboard Jungle* was published, the writer met with an editor at Pocket Books to discuss writing a series for them. He told the editor that "the only valid people to deal with crime were cops, and I would like to make the lead character, rather than a single person, a squad of cops instead—so it would be a conglomerate lead character."[12]

Pocket agreed to publish three books, with more to follow if they were successful. The debut of McBain's police procedural 87th Precinct series, 1956's *Cop Hater*, reflected the author's "months in research in the precincts, in the cars, in the courts, and at the labs before I wrote the first book."[13] Set in Isola, a metropolis similar to New York City, the series offers a number of protagonists, with Detective Steve Carrella appearing the most often.

Author and screenwriter Evan Hunter is seen here in August 1976. Born Salvatore Lombino, he legally adopted the name Evan Hunter in 1952 because he was afraid his Italian-American heritage would scare off prospective publishers. While successful as Evan Hunter, he was even more famous as Ed McBain, a name he used for most of his crime fiction, including the 87th Precinct series.

Celebrated for its gritty authenticity in its depictions of police work, the series was groundbreaking. The author would continue to write one to two novels in the series every year, along with more literary novels as Evan Hunter, until his death in 2005.

HIDE AND SEEK

Unlike these authors, Jacqueline Wilson did not set out to write a crime novel as her first adult work. "[*Hide and Seek*] was about the kidnapping of two little girls and when Macmillan heard that my then husband was a policeman they were even more excited because they thought that I would be able to write police procedurals for them," Jacqueline Wilson remembered. "But the very last thing in the world I wanted to do was write about the police services, because I had enough of that in my own domestic circumstances."[14]

Hide and Seek follows the kidnapping from multiple perspectives, focusing mainly on the points of view of the mother of one girl, 29-year-old Rose, who was recently separated from her husband; her eight-year-old daughter, Alice; and the girl's kidnapper. It was a suspense thriller written for adults, with several sections that would be considered too graphic and disturbing for most of her younger readers.

"I did check with [my husband] occasionally on specific details of police procedure, but mostly my novels were more about the people committing the crimes—they were sort of 'why they did it' rather than 'who done it,'" Wilson explained, adding, "Lots of people did seem to assume that my husband would have given me some of the ideas, which I rather resented bitterly because I'm not even sure if he read them."[15]

For her debut novel, her husband did, however, lend his name. The officer assigned to investigate the kidnapping, Detective Inspector Rob Millar's last name was William Wilson's middle one. "He might have noticed that,"

Wilson concedes, "but he certainly wasn't a great reader
. . . he wasn't against my writing career, but it didn't spe-
cifically connect with him at all."[16]

Kidnapper Norman, a 19-year-old grocery clerk, may
have been unlikable, but Wilson portrayed him with sym-
pathy by highlighting the character's numerous challenges.
Readers of Wilson's debut novel found many elements
which later appeared in her books for younger audiences.
For instance, Alice's mother was recently separated. Growing up, Wilson's own family remained intact, but she drew
upon her experiences while enduring their quarrels. Her
protagonists are often raised by single parents (both mothers and fathers). And just as it had been in Wilson's own
home, money was often an issue. In *Hide and Seek*, Rose
must work in order to provide for her daughter.

Wilson, and many readers, felt that her most authentic
character in *Hide and Seek* was eight-year-old Alice. A
bright girl who wears glasses (much like Wilson at eight),
she was not an idealized young heroine like many of those
in books Wilson read as a child. Alice could be mean and
bratty. She used vulgar language. Her only friend is a child
half her age who she often bosses around. She also seems
quite worldly.

Over the next five years, Wilson authored four other
crime novels, *Truth or Dare*; *Snap*; *Let's Pretend*; and
Making Hate. "I wrote five crime novels for adults," she
later explained, "but each one had a child as one of the
major characters and I knew I didn't really want to write
about crime at all, I wanted to write about children."[17]

By the time *Making Hate* was published in 1977, Jacqueline Wilson had completed a novel for young adults. There
was only one problem. No one wanted to publish it.

Jacqueline Wilson launched a new career for herself when she realized that the book she had written, Nobody's Perfect, was in fact a story for young readers. Since that time, she had written young adult literature almost exclusively. Seen here, Wilson launches World Book Day, the largest annual celebration of books and reading in the United Kingdom, on March 2, 2006.

6

A New Career

JACQUELINE WILSON'S WRITING was often inspired by what she has read. A newspaper advertisement led to her first writing job. A visit to the library led to her first book for young adults. And after reading an article about a child's quest to find her birth parents, Wilson realized she had a story for young readers.

Although she wrote a children's book called *Ricky's Birthday*, her other books had been crime thrillers intended for adults. But they shared a common element: Every one of them featured a young person, either as a main character or in a

79

supporting role. To Wilson, they were the most interesting and most authentic of her characters.

Her first book for middle readers, *Nobody's Perfect*, describes main character Sandra's quest to find the biological father who abandoned her. When Wilson began writing it, she wanted an audience of younger readers. The novelist remarked in an interview, "I do write some novels for teenagers, but most of my work is aimed at seven to fourteen year olds. I think I particularly like writing about nine, ten and eleven year olds because I have such vivid memories of being that age myself."[1]

Although Wilson had written five novels for adults in five years, it took her another five years to find a publisher willing to take a risk on her book for middle readers. Why did that happen? Writers who become successful in one genre or facet of publishing are not always immediately successful in another. Indeed, for Wilson, getting *Nobody's Perfect* published was scarcely easier than it would have been if she had never written a novel before. "Macmillan themselves didn't particularly care for it and so it had to go the rounds," the author remembered. It was rejected by several more publishers, "but eventually Oxford University press accepted it."[2]

The publication of *Nobody's Perfect* immediately altered Wilson's career. The book earned her decent reviews and the beginnings of a fan base. Writing in *Books for Keeps*, critic Steve Bowles noted *Nobody's Perfect* was "one of the more readable books [for younger readers], dealing with conflict with mother and stepfather, sibling rivalry, a blind date, the beginnings of love and Sandra's search for her real father."[3]

From the beginning, the books Wilson wrote for children were radically different than most other books in that category. The language was fairly simple, but the ideas could be quite complex. Her main characters were not yet teens, but they often had to be independent, taking care of not only themselves but their mothers or fathers as well.

Wilson's audience was middle readers, ages eight to 12 years old. Her novels usually featured a main character, often a girl, in that age group. Although books for middle readers had dealt with subjects like death and divorce before, the realistic manner in which Wilson dealt with them was unusual. And while she wrote for middle readers, in many aspects her work resembled books written for young adults.

PROBLEM NOVELS

Young adult books are marketed to readers as young as 10 or as old as 18. They generally (although not always) have a protagonist in that age group and are usually less than 300 pages long. There are numerous books with young protagonists that are fairly short, but young adult books are actually *marketed* to that age group. In the 1800s, a number of novels including *Adventures of Huckleberry Finn*, *Little Women*, and *Treasure Island* featured young main characters and were embraced by younger readers. Despite the popularity of such novels, publishers were slow to produce books for young adults.

Before the early 1900s, the period between childhood and adulthood was brief. Less than 10 percent of adults graduated high school; women were only rarely educated past the eighth grade. In their mid-teens, young men often had jobs, either on farms or in factories. Before marriage, many women also worked in menial jobs. Most started families before they reached 20 years of age.

During the Great Depression of the 1930s, jobs disappeared and public high schools grew in number. "This shift away from disparate jobs to mass education," notes author K.L. Going, "allowed adolescents to take on an identity as a group, and people began to look at them differently. Young people now had more opportunity to relate to each other, and they gradually began to define themselves through their music, fashion and beliefs."[4]

As greater numbers of young adults were educated, publishers began producing books for them. Most of the books produced at that time appealed to the younger end of the spectrum, works like *Rebecca of Sunnybrook Farm* and *My Friend Flicka*. In the 1940s, what many consider the first young adult novel with an authentic teen voice, Maureen Daly's *Seventeenth Summer*, was published.

It was also in the 1940s that advertisers began referring to potential customers between the ages of 13 and 19 as "teenagers." The teenagers who came of age in the 1940s and 1950s grew up to write novels radically different from the ones that they had read as young adults. They wrote about how the dreams and values of teens often conflicted with adults. They addressed issues avoided in earlier works, including pregnancy, gang violence, drugs, and sexuality.

S.E. Hinton, a teenager herself when she wrote 1967's *The Outsiders*, described the sometimes-violent conflicts between the well-off "Socs" and the poorer "Greasers" in Oklahoma. In 1970, Judy Blume's *Are You There God? Its Me, Margaret* offered a sixth-grade girl dealing with her changing body, her relationship to God, and the challenges she faced from difficult friends. As young adult author Meg Cabot notes, "The most delightful thing about

Many books have inspired Jacqueline Wilson's work as a children's author, but few more than J.D. Salinger's The Catcher in the Rye. *Salinger, seen here, is considered one of the best American authors of the mid-twentieth century.*

Judy Blume's books is that unlike so many other children's books, they never feature a sage adult offering wise counsel in their time of need. . . . [The characters] simply go on living. Just like the rest of us."[5]

From Blume's books to Willo Davis Robert's novel of child abuse, *Don't Hurt Laurie*, and coauthor's Paul Zindel and Crescent Dragonwagon's tale of a teenage runaway, *To Take a Dare*, young adult novels of the 1970s and 1980s found a growing audience. These books were not just being read by young adults; in England, crime writer Jacqueline Wilson noticed them as well. "I got interested in the way American teenage novels were developing," she explained to *School Library Journal* in 2006. "There were lots in the '70s told as first-person narratives and I liked this colloquial, open style."[6]

Yet while they were championed for their authentic point of view (usually directly from the protagonist's eyes) and the way they were written (as teens actually spoke), some critics attacked these works. "This tendency to focus on harsh realities was both a blessing and a curse for YA literature," notes K.L. Going. "The books [from the 1970s and 1980s] broke down boundaries for acceptable subject

Did you know...

Many novels, including Sylvia Plath's *The Bell Jar* and J.D. Salinger's *The Catcher in the Rye*, inspired Jacqueline Wilson's work as a writer for young people. Both books focus on troubled main characters who end up in mental institutions.

matter and language, and they gave teens a voice of their own, but many of them also gave rise to the stigma of teen books as 'problem novels'—undeveloped stories . . . that focused on issues rather than literary merit."[7]

In reviews of Wilson's books for younger readers, they are occasionally called "problem novels." Yet from her debut work, she avoided the easy dismissal of such a label; reviewing *Nobody's Perfect*, Zena Sutherland offers that the "characterization, plot and pace all have impact" while the treatment of the relationships in the book was "realistic and perceptive."[8] That realism allowed Wilson to quit the anonymous magazine writing she loathed for a full-time career as a novelist.

CAREER IN THE 1980s

The discipline Wilson developed while writing 10,000 words of magazine fiction every week served her well. She began writing one to two books for young readers every year; it is a pace she has continued for almost three decades. After the publication of *Nobody's Perfect*, she was able to focus on a career as a novelist. "It was hard work," Wilson remembered, but she was able to make a decent living. [9]

Like many of her novels, 1984's *The Other Side*, drew on her recollections of childhood. As a young girl, Wilson believed if she stared hard enough at the ceiling that she would be able to float up over her bed. *The Other Side*'s main character does not just imagine levitating, she does it. The question, the reader asks, is it all a dream?

When divorce became commonplace in the 1970s and 1980s, Wilson's novels reflected that changing reality. In *How to Survive Summer Camp*, Stella is sent to camp while her mother embarks on a honeymoon with her second husband. Though *This Girl* and *The Dream Palace* were marketed to slightly older readers, they covered similar ground. *This Girl* shows what happens when main character Coral leaves her home for a job as a nanny. *The Dream Palace* portrays protagonist Lolly's life at home with a mother and stepfather, and with new boyfriend Greg who lives with squatters—people who live in abandoned buildings. "Teenage readers will be engrossed and challenged by this unputdownable, skillfully crafted book," offered one of many complimentary reviews of *The Dream Palace*.[10]

As *Daily Telegraph* writer Cassandra Jandine notes, Wilson's protagonists often have "unkind stepfathers or drunken mothers, [mean] friends and broken hearts, they experience death and divorce but they come through—and never lose their sense of humor."[11]

Though Wilson attracted a growing audience through the 1980s, she began to see challenges as well. "In the seventies and eighties, you seemed to have more freedom to write all sorts of different things, and I did rather enjoy writing these serious teenage novels but they were very much for a specific audience," Wilson remembered.[12]

The author wanted to reach a larger audience. She recalled, "When I started to go out to schools and give talks about my books I realized that maybe they only appealed to about ten percent of introverted, would-be writers. I thought well, maybe there's a way of writing books where I don't exactly dumb down but present them in a more immediate way so that the sort [of] kids who don't generally like reading books can be interested in them too."[13]

By 1990, Wilson had changed publishers. When she approached Transworld (which would become part of

Random House), she offered them a novel intended for a broader audience. It would not only be more successful than she could have imagined, it would also make her as polarizing an author as Judy Blume had ever been.

Jacqueline Wilson signs copies of her latest book for a group of young girls. She is one of those rare young adult novelists who is both critically acclaimed and enormously popular.

7

Household Name

MANY WRITERS NEVER sell their first novel. A novel-ist's "first book" is often his or her fourth or fifth, with unsold manuscripts frequently stacked in a closet or hidden inside a file cabinet. Jacqueline Wilson was no different. By the time *Hide or Seek* was published, she had written and tucked away several unpublished efforts.

Just as a writer's first book is generally not published, few earn very much from their first sale. Many writers never make a living as novelists. First-time novelists generally receive advances of less than $10,000. The advance is money paid against royalties—a small percentage of each book's price. Most manuscripts take a year from acceptance to publication. After that, many books never sell well enough for the author to pay back the advance; even if they do it can be months, even years, before they receive a royalty check.

"Gary Paulsen, one of the most famous YA authors today, wrote many adult novels and lived close to the poverty level for many years before one of his YA novels won a Newbery Medal and brought his talent into the limelight," notes Sherry Garland in *Writing for Young Adults*. "The majority of YA authors (or most authors for that matter) are not able to support themselves by writing."[1]

Novelists not only teach, they also work as reporters or librarians or have some other "day job." A few have rich spouses. Wilson was blessed. While her early novels were not best sellers, they contributed a decent sum to her family's income. Still, by the early 1990s, she had not achieved all her childhood dreams—she was a writer, yes, but not a famous one interviewed on chat shows and in newspaper articles.

ENTER TRACY BEAKER

The Story of Tracy Beaker was a life-changing book for Wilson. Like Katherine Paterson's *A Bridge to Terabithia*, Lois Lowry's *The Giver*, and Gary Paulsen's *Dogsong*, it became Wilson's best-known work. It inspired two sequels, *The Dare Game* in 2000, and *Starring Tracy Beaker* in 2006, along with two television programs. Nearly two decades after it was published, the novel continues to be widely read, often by the children of its original audience.

The Story of Tracy Beaker also represented a stylistic departure for Wilson. Many modern authors strive to utilize as much "white space" as possible—the portions of the page that are not covered by words. In adult novels this is accomplished by dialogue and short paragraphs. Wilson had a different method. "I wanted lots of illustrations," she told *School Library Journal*, "because I thought they would break up the text and maybe attract readers who would be put off reading dense wording. I also thought it would be very much a part of the book to have Tracy doing all her little drawings.[2]

Inspired by books by Noel Streatfeild and Eve Garnett, which she had read as a child, she asked her publisher Transworld if they thought it would be possible to include illustrations. They were "very sweet and said yes, you can have Nick Sharratt and there we go! That's what happened."[3]

Sharratt would become a regular collaborator, illustrating almost all of her books from then on. *Contemporary Authors Online* notes that "Sharratt's cartoon-like illustrations are a good compliment for Wilson's style, reviewers have generally remarked."[4] Adding his drawings to *The Story of Tracy Beaker* also helped to lighten some of the darker sections of the book.

"Now Nick and I are such a sort of artistic team, I don't think I could really contemplate doing a book unless Nick was illustrating it," Wilson explains. "I find it quite sad because for whatever reason the American editions, many of them have not got Nick Sharratt covers. In this country, and certainly many others, they seem so much a part of the book, but that's something you just have to deal with—what works in one country doesn't necessarily work in another."[5]

Although she had only experimented with the first-person point of view before, it would become her dominant style from *The Story of Tracy Beaker* on. Presenting the 10-year-old main character's viewpoint offered readers insight into her feelings and experiences. Its raw immediacy was one reason the author utilized it. "First person is conversational," explains K.L. Going in *Writing & Selling the YA Novel*. "The character is talking directly to the reader, so right from the start the reader and the character have an implied relationship . . . in first person the narrating character and the reader connect, and this makes first person feel intimate."[6]

At the beginning of the novel, Tracy explains, "I lived with my mom when I was little and we got on great but then she got this Monster Gorilla Boyfriend and I hated him and he hated me back and beat me up so I had to be taken away to a children's home. No wonder my mom sent him packing."[7]

Tracy lives in a children's home, having been abandoned by her mother and returned to the home by two sets of foster parents. She dreams of a new foster family and even writes an imaginary classified advertisement: "very rich parents preferred as little Tracy needs lots of toys, presents and pets to make up for her tragic past."[8]

Unfolding in the form of a journal, the novel provides Tracy's side of events as she details her fights with another girl at the children's home and her slow acceptance of a boy who insists on liking her. "Even when the narrator is telling what happened to her, not every sentence can begin with I," Going cautions in her book, "and dialogue and action must still be your primary tools for advancing the plot."[9]

The Story of Tracy Beaker manages to utilize both dialogue and action despite its format. Describing Tracy as "bitingly funny, amusingly bitter, and at odds with the world," *Booklist* reviewer Ilene Cooper writes that "Tracy's heartache and the bravado she musters to cover it will be readily identifiable by readers, who will appreciate both her honesty and her wit."[10]

The story avoids presenting Tracy as immediately likeable or kindhearted. She bears less resemblance to the main character in *Oliver Twist* than Mary from *The Secret Garden*. Published in 1909, the latter novel has been cited by a number of contemporary novelists, including Wilson, Paterson, and Lowry, who were inspired by reading it as children. On its first page, Mary is described as "the most disagreeable child ever seen . . . with a thin little face and a thin little body, thin light hair and a sour expression."[11]

Shelf Discovery author Lizzie Skurnick humorously asserts that "somewhere along the line, along with straw prams and caning rods, having a child character not even the narrator could stand went out of business."[12] Yet Wilson does not shrink from describing Tracy's bad qualities: She lies and steals and punches another girl in the nose. Tracy describes herself as "ugly" and behaves in an ugly fashion, yet one reviewer noted that "underneath the brashness and bravado is a desperately unhappy, self-deluding, insecure personality."[13]

An aspiring writer, Tracy not only finds escape through her journal but also uses it to connect with a published writer. When she visits the children's home, Tracy shares her writing and begins to see a woman there as a potential rescuer—at least until her absent mother arrives. Instead of a traditional happy ending where the loose ends are neatly tied up, the book offers a more open-ended conclusion.

BACKLASH

The Story of Tracy Beaker represented a major departure for Jacqueline Wilson. "It was more immediate," she remembered. "It was aimed at a slightly younger audience. It was perhaps shorter."[14] She also recalled, "Everything came together and I found I could expect the sort of things I wanted to and be as immediate as I wanted to and in that kind of way. . . I suddenly discovered the way I wanted to write."[15]

The author had little indication of the book's potential; its eventual success transformed Wilson to a name brand.

Tracy Beaker because so popular that her image adorned lunch pails and T-shirts. "So this is lovely," Wilson told *School Library Journal*, "but it's also more work because I'm a control freak and I want to make sure everything looks attractive and that children are going to be getting value for their money."[16]

Besides the books and merchandising, the novel became a television series. Airing on CBBC, the British Broadcasting Corporation's children's channel, *The Story of Tracy Beaker*, aired for five seasons. "[A]lthough [*The Story of Tracy Beaker*] was optioned for a television series," Wilson explained, "it was I think a good ten years before they actually made the television series, and since then it's become a very successful television series on British television . . . and now in this country, Tracy Beaker is kind of a household name."[17] In some respects, the process was as long and as challenging as getting a novel published. "Initially I wanted to be very involved and indeed I was, but television teams change very rapidly," Wilson goes on. "Slowly the key people change, different people come on board, different writers come on board and try as you can you don't stay the driving force behind it and it's almost as if its taken off under its own steam now."[18]

Did you know...

Actress Dani Harmer portrayed Tracy Beaker in both *The Story of Tracy Beaker*, which aired from 2002 to 2007 and its spin-off, *Tracy Beaker Returns*, which premiered in 2010. The spin-off followed the former foster child as an adult returning to work at the children's home where she once lived.

The show was viewed by younger children who may not have read the books. One mother described how her eight-year-old son quoted it by saying, "No one likes me," and "This is the worst thing that has ever happened to me." She complained that "the form Wilson pioneers where kindly adults are constantly exposed as lacking and relentlessly bested and undermined by fearless, victimized children accounts for a good deal of the tension in otherwise stable middle-class homes."[19]

Presenting occasionally grim topics to younger readers opened Wilson up to numerous attacks from critics, parents, and librarians. Interviewed by *Publishers Weekly* in 2007, Wilson's American publisher Beverly Horowitz at Bantam Doubleday Dell noted, "Ten years ago the gate-keepers of the children's book world were a little more cautious about the content of Jacky Wilson's books than perhaps they would be now. Jacky deals with things like eating disorders, problems that she doesn't necessarily feel she can solve, but she does bring it up. In a YA novel that's fine."[20]

But for middle readers such lack of resolution can be more problematic. Wilson agrees her books do not have easy resolutions: "If you're going to get a sort of unpleasant stepdad, he's not generally in my books going to change his ways, and suddenly become Mr. Happy and Delightful. . . . There is resolution, but it isn't exactly the way a traditional story works out."[21]

Wilson's readability, to some critics, was a significant part of the flaw. Winifred Robinson complained in the *Daily Mail* that Wilson's books are

> written simply enough for an eight-year-old to read aloud and I doubt that any young child really needs to explore at length the nitty gritty of redundancy, bereavement and divorce.

British actress Dani Harmer poses at the EA British Academy Children's Awards at the London Hilton in London, England, on November 29, 2009. Harmer portrayed Jacqueline Wilson's character Tracy Beaker in two television series.

I understand that specialist books exploring the topics can be immensely useful to children unlucky enough to have direct experience of such traumas. But for the rest, I strongly suspect it opens the door to experiences from which they should be protected for as long as possible so that childhood innocence can be preserved rather than overshadowed by too much sophisticated knowledge presented too early and little understood.[22]

The "rest," as Robinson puts it, may be a more troubled group than she suspects. From book signings and appearances, letters and e-mails (the latter printed out, for Wilson does not have e-mail at her home), the author feels intimately connected to her readers. Their correspondence, she believes, "certainly reflects all the modern life problems. I want to show children that I understand that they're not alone, that lots of people have moms and dads who can't get along, or various types of problems in their lives . . . my books can make them feel that there are other people going through the types of things they are."[23]

Still, although she does not shy away from controversy, Wilson also feels that she has a certain responsibility because of her now wider audience. "In my teenage novels I had characters doing things that probably I wouldn't have them doing now and it slightly complicates matters because quite young children read my books nowadays," Wilson admits. She finds that any "adult content" has to be handled quite carefully or else, as she says, "I get into trouble in the press for it."[24]

By her late fifties, Wilson was the most borrowed author in British libraries (surpassing even Harry Potter writer J.K. Rowling). She has written more than 90 titles and has sold more than 25 million books in her home country. Yet there remained an unconquered territory: the United States of America.

Here, Jacqueline Wilson and artist, curator, and teacher Richard Wentworth are announced as the first Foundling Fellows at the Foundling Museum in central London. In recent years, Wilson has received a number of awards for her writing.

8

Conquering America

LIKE A PARENT with more than one child, authors of multiple books have a hard time selecting their favorite. Still, out of all of Jacqueline Wilson's modern novels (as of late 2010 more than 90 of them) there is one that stands out for Wilson. "I generally choose *The Illustrated Mum* because I tried particularly hard with that book and felt so sorry for poor little Dolphin [the novel's main character]," Wilson offered in her memoir *Jacky Daydream*.[1]

The book began during a walk in a park. It was in New York City, after a day of shopping and touring the Metropolitan

Museum of Art with her daughter, Emma. The two were sitting on the grass, eating ice cream, she remembered:

> We watched a very unusual arty looking young woman saun-
> tering along. She had many intricate tattoos on her arms and
> legs, even on her neck. There were two girls with her, in rather
> ragged dressing up clothes, tottering in borrowed high heeled
> sandals. When they were out of earshot Emma said to me,
> "Don't they look like the sort of family you'd write about in
> one of your books!" I made a note about them there and then in
> my diary—and not long after, I started *The Illustrated Mum*.[2]

Told from the point of view of 11-year-old Dolphin (or Dol as she is known), the story traces the emotional roller-coaster ride her mother puts her on. An untreated manic-depressive, her mother, Marigold, celebrates every occasion with a new tattoo, until nearly her entire body has been covered with them. They live in a council home not too dissimilar from the one where Wilson grew up. Marigold also has difficulty with money and relationships, and is particularly obsessed with the father of Dol's 14-year-old sister, Star. When Micky shows up, he soon convinces Star to live with him in relative affluence. Meanwhile, Marigold descends into near madness, and Dol struggles to take care of her mother and keep her out of a hospital while trying to dodge foster care.

"If you have a parent with some kind of mental problems, to you they're just your mum who you love tremendously much but sometimes she can be a bit scary or unreliable," the author explained in an interview. "You don't think nec-essarily in terms of, right, what is this diagnosis and all the rest of it. I wanted to show what life can be like for kids in this sort of situation."[3]

"Wilson, who always writes realistically and with humor, outdoes herself in this story," Ilene Cooper wrote in a 2005 *Booklist* review. "Star is convincing as the worried, responsible sister who longs to move out and feels guilty about it, and Dolphin never seems older than her years as she relates the alternating awe and fear that everyone around her inspires."[4]

Looking back on the novel, the author told *School Library Journal* that, "I knew I was doing something quite difficult, writing about a much-loved mother who lets her children down and suffers from mental illness and behaves very irresponsibly. I knew it was going to be a book without many laughs because there's just no way you could have a sense of humor about such a searing and worrying subject."[5]

GIRLS

The sequel to *The Story of Tracy Beaker*, *The Dare Game*, was a surprise for the author, who had not anticipated

Did you know...

The title of *The Illustrated Mum* was inspired by one of Jacqueline Wilson's favorite books, Ray Bradbury's short story collection *The Illustrated Man*, which was first published in 1951. The man in the title is covered with tattoos, which were allegedly created by a woman from the future. Throughout the course of the book, each comes to life and tells a different tale.

writing more about Tracy. She recalled, "I got so many letters from children asking what happened next to her. . . . If
you invent a strong character they don't go away."[6]

Her Girls series, however, was more designed. "I wanted
to show exactly what it is like to be a teenage girl," Wilson
explained. "What it's like when you feel that you're the
slightly plain one of your friends."[7]

In the first few pages of *Bad Girls*, a stand-alone novel,
protagonist Mandy White is assaulted by several girls and
subsequently hit by a bus. On the other hand, the opening of
the first book in the Girls series, *Girls in Love*, spends nearly
20 pages inside the head of main character Elle as she walks
to school. "It depends on the book," Wilson offered, "sometimes I like to have lots of dramatic events, sometimes I'm
more interested in the sort of emotional situation. I don't
sort of plot it out beforehand, as I start thinking about the
characters, that's the way the books develop."[8]

Girls in Love offered a character familiar to readers of
Wilson's earlier novels. Protagonist Elle crafts an imaginary romance with a geeky younger boy she befriended on
a vacation in Wales, substituting the looks of an older man
she sees on the way to school. Dan, despite not being her
physical type, saves the day when skinheads crash a party
Elle is attending and later provides her first real kiss.

Wilson's experiences with Cookie and Colin when she
was a teenager on holiday informed a number of her novels.
Her characters, however, often wound up with the socially
awkward, geeky boys rather than the good-looking best
friend, as she had done. In both *Tracy Beaker* and *The Illustrated Mum*, the girl becomes friends with an unlikely boy.

Writing about the Girls series in *Contemporary Writers*,
Liz O'Reilly noted, "These books are aimed at a slightly
older age-group (early teens) but, paradoxically, they tackle

less serious issues than some of the pre-teen books. On the whole [the characters in the series] do not suffer from the more extreme fears and crises experienced by Tracy Beaker, Dolphin and other characters."[9]

While it may not have been as "serious" as some of her other novels, Wilson explained, "Lots and lots of girls have enjoyed this series and identified totally with my main girl and they all want to know what's going to happen next. I have written four of them and they are probably a little dated now and I really feel four is enough."[10]

U.S.A.

In the summer of 2002, Jacqueline Wilson admitted to *Publishers Weekly*, "It sounds very greedy, but I would love to be as popular in America as I am in the U.K." The author has visited Boston, Massachusetts, nearly every year and was looking forward to going for a book tour: "It's nice to be sent there to do some work."[11]

Although she toured the United States, extensively promoting *Girls Out Late*, the third in the series, her books were nowhere near as popular in the United States as they were in England. Four years later, she switched publishers, leaving Random House's Delacorte for the small publisher Roaring Brook Press. The latter publisher, launched in 2002, hoped to improve upon her U.S. sales, which at that point were approximately 600,000 total for the 11 titles published over the previous 10 years by Random House.

Her first title for Roaring Brook was *Candyfloss*. Wilson remembered the source of the inspiration was when she was giving autographs and noticed a man with "a chip van and he said when [his daughter] stayed with him, which let me know he didn't have her fulltime, she would read my books in the back of the van while he was working. That seemed so tender to me, and it gave me the idea for the relationship between Floss and her dad."[12]

In the book, Floss's dad owns a chip shop, selling fried potatoes and chip butty—rolls that are buttered and filled with French fries. His business has declined, partly because of the movement toward healthier eating. Despite her father's uncertain circumstances, Floss chooses to stay with him instead of going to Australia to live for six months with her mother and her new, upper-middle-class husband.

In a review of the book, *Publishers Weekly* noted the numerous exciting parts of the novel, including a fight and a fire: "All that action makes the narrative longer than usual for this age group, but Floss's emotional turmoil should hook girls. There's a real tenderness to her relationship with her father, fully dimensional in all his flaws, a man whose love for his daughter often clouds his judgment."[13]

The review also noted the illustrations by Nick Sharratt, which open each chapter. But unlike the Sharratt covers that had adorned Wilson's novels in Britain, the cover of *Candyfloss* was a simple photograph. To some in the United States, the change was a good one. "Kids here are very sophisticated and cover art is extremely important," Becky Anderson, owner of Anderson's Bookshops in Naperville, Illinois, argued. "The artwork was just too babyish and, even more important than that, I don't think it reflected what the stories were about."[14]

Wilson understood the changes. "I think Roaring Brook is trying hard to make me better known in America, and I have to respect that and be grateful for it," the author explained in a recent interview. "I did fight quite fiercely on Nick's behalf but you know I don't see the point in carrying on a battle when you know you're not going to win."[15] Still, despite the change in publishers and covers,

Dame Jacqueline Wilson is photographed with the insignia of her new title, which she collected from Queen Elizabeth II during an investiture ceremony at Buckingham Palace in London.

Wilson admitted, "I don't know what the sales are. I would imagine that if they had been an enormous success Roaring Brook and I would be clinking our champagne glasses together."[16]

She sees the challenge partly because of the size of the country, where books may sell well on the coasts and not in the Midwest or vice versa. "I don't think it's a problem that my books are too British, I think they just haven't quite hit the right nerve in America." Indeed, *Candyfloss* offered a "Floss's Gloss" in the back—a glossary offering translations of common British words and phrases.[17]

AWARDS AND CHALLENGES

Wilson served as Children's Laureate from 2005 to 2007, a position awarded to a distinguished writer or illustrator of children's books in Great Britain. In 2007, she was made a Dame Commander of the British Empire—the female equivalent of a knight. The title was given by the queen but was based upon the choice of a committee based on nominations made by the government and the general public.

Unfortunately, poor health almost kept her from attending the Buckingham Palace ceremony. Besides writing as many as three books a year, Wilson is an avid swimmer, completing 50 laps nearly every morning. If anything, she appears thinner than she did in her teens. Despite her healthy lifestyle, the author nearly died from heart failure in 2008.

"I remember thinking, 'Bloody hell, this'll be curtains, immediately,'" she told the London *Guardian* in the summer of 2010. "But thank goodness for modern drugs, and I've got a gadget in my chest—if I should fail utterly—it apparently has the kick of a mule. But, you know—you have absolutely no idea whether you've got an ordinary life span left. Common sense tells you you probably haven't."[18]

INTO THE FUTURE

Despite those challenges, the writer continues to write, and is closing in on her one-hundredth novel. "I have my own study which I go into and I can work there," she explained in a 2010 interview. "Nowadays in the morning, the first thing I do when I get up is I lie on the sofa and before I'm even up and dressed I write again there. . . . I'm lucky enough to be able to write anywhere at all."[19]

Many of her books have begun on a train, written in notebooks as she traveled around London. She can usually manage 500 words while traveling, with another 500 at home. She admits to missing, or even deliberately skipping, a stop to finish an important section.

While she prefers writing in "pretty notebooks, I've been known to write on the backs of envelopes or any paper that's handy you know if I haven't got my notebook with me and I suddenly have half-an-hour to kill."[20] And she continues to experiment as a writer. Although she dabbled with historical sections in novels like *The Lottie Project*, her first historical novel was *Hetty Feather*, which was first published in 2009. Set in the 1880s, the book represented a radical departure for a writer whose work had exclusively dealt with contemporary settings. "I thought it would be a bit of a challenge," she admitted in an online interview, "but I love the period and thought I'd give it a go."[21]

Written over a six-month period as she recuperated from heart surgery, she had no idea whether or not it would appeal to her regular readers:

> I did wonder if this might prove a problem, however it was sort of tied in with the [Thomas Coram] Foundling Museum at London, and they were delighted that I was doing this novel, and I had the lucky launch party there. And it has been surprisingly successful.

And lots of girls who don't necessarily read historical novels have taken Hetty to their hearts, surprisingly. I think it helps that the book is written still in the first person and it's a Victorian novel, but its familiar territory to girls who feel hard done by.[22]

More than 50 years ago, 11-year-old Jacky Aitken crept out of her family's hotel room in Bournemouth and made her way to the seashore. There she watched the waves and felt overwhelmed with the need to make a wish. In that perfect moment, it seemed as if wishes could come true. She thought of all the wishes she could make and discarded them one by one. So she made the same wish she did over her birthday candles, beneath the first star of evening or pulling apart the wishbone of a turkey. She wished to be a writer and have a book published someday.

Fifty years later, writer Jacqueline Wilson knows that little girl "wouldn't have believed it possible that one day I'd have ninety books published, not just one. I'd laugh at the idea that one amazing day children would queue up outside a book shop in Bournemouth for eight hours simply so I could sign their books. My books."[23]

CHRONOLOGY

1945 Jacqueline Aitken is born on December 17 in Bath, England, to Harry and Margaret Aitken.

1947–1949 Jacky lives with her parents at her grandparents' house on 38 Fassett Road in Kingston-on-Thames, England.

1949–1951 Harry and Margaret move with Jacky to two rented rooms in Lewisham, England.

1951 Jacky's family moves into Cumberland House on Kingston Hill.

1953 Jacky's parents buy a new 11-inch television to watch the coronation of Queen Elizabeth II.

1954 Jacky enters the Latchmere Primary School in Kingston.

1957 Jacky enters Coombe County Secondary School for Girls.

1962 Leaves Coombe County School; begins training to be a secretary.

1963 Begins working as a freelance writer for D.C. Thomson.

1963–1965 Hired as a full-time writer, she relocates to Dundee, Scotland. Writes for a number of Thomson's magazines, including *Jackie*.

1965 Marries William Millar Wilson on August 28.

1967 Daughter Emma Fiona is born on February 16.

1972 *Hide and Seek*, a novel for adults, is published.

1973 *Ricky's Birthday*, a novel for young children, is published.

1982 *Nobody's Perfect*, a novel for middle readers, is published.

1991 *The Story of Tracy Beaker* is published.

1996 Separates from husband; divorces in 2004.

2005–2007 Named Children's Laureate.

2007 Named Dame Commander, Order of the British Empire.

2008 Suffers heart failure but recovers.

2009 *Hetty Feather*, her first historical novel, is published.

2010 *The Longest Whale Song* and *Little Darlings* are published.

NOTES

Chapter 1

1 Louise Johncox, "Interview with Jacqueline Wilson," (London) *Sunday Times*, November 2, 2003, p. 3.

2 Rosanna Greenstreet, "Jacqueline Wilson on *Jackie* Magazine," (London) *Guardian*, September 5, 2009.

3 Aida Edemarian, "Jacqueline Wilson: The Grande Dame of Girlhood," (London) *Guardian*, July 10, 2010.

4 Ibid.

5 "Jacqueline Kennedy Onassis," *Newsmakers 1994*, Issue 4. Gale Research.

6 Edemarian, "Wilson: Grande Dame."

Chapter 2

1 Edemarian, "Wilson: Grande Dame."

2 "BBC-History-Britain bombs Berlin (pictures, video, facts & news)." BBC Homepage. http://www.bbc.co.uk/history/events/britain_bombs_berlin.

3 Jacqueline Wilson, telephone interview with John Bankston, October 19, 2010.

4 "Adolf Hitler," *Historic World Leaders*. Gale Biography In Context. http://www.gale.cengage.com/InContext/bio.htm.

5 Neville Chamberlain, "Peace for Our Time"—Speech given on September 20, 1938, *Sources of British History*.

6 "England in the 20th Century," Part 8, World War II. Britannia.com. http://www.britannia.com/history/nar20hist4.html.

7 Ibid.

8 Jacqueline Wilson, "My Mum and Dad," *Jacky Daydream*. New York: Doubleday UK, 2007, p. 10.

9 Wilson, Bankston telephone interview.

10 "World War Two in Europe." The History Place. http://www.historyplace.com/worldwar2/timeline/pearl.htm.

11 Jacqueline Wilson, "My Family," *My Secret Diary: Dating, Dancing, Dreams and Dilemmas*. London: Corgi, 2010, p. 13.

12 Edemarian, "Wilson: Grande Dame."

13 Wilson, Bankston telephone interview.

14 Ibid.

15 Wilson, "Cumberland House," *Jacky Daydream*, p. 105.

16 Wilson, Bankston telephone interview.

17 Wilson, "Latchmere Infants," *Jacky Daydream*, p. 119.

18 Ibid., p. 120.

19 Ibid., p. 121.

20 Ibid., "Mandy," pp. 156–157.

21 Ibid., "Biddy," p. 189.

22 Edemarian, "Wilson: Grande Dame."

23 Wilson, "Mr. Townsend," *Jacky Daydream*, p. 262.

24 Ibid., p. 266.

25 Ibid., "The Coronation," p. 167.

26 Ibid., "Mr. Townsend," p. 268.

27 Ibid.

28 Ibid., p. 271.

29 Ibid.

30 Ibid., p. 273.

31 Ibid., p. 274.

32 "Books," pp. 210–211.

Chapter 3

1 Wilson, "School," *My Secret Diary*, p. 127.

2 Wilson, "Mr. Branson," *Jacky Daydream*, p. 281.

3 Ibid.

4 Ibid., "The Eleven Plus," p. 285.

5 Ibid., p. 286.

6 Ibid., p. 288.

7 Ibid.

8 Ibid., p. 290.

9 Wilson, "Chris," *My Secret Diary*, p. 42.

10 Ibid., "School," p. 127.

11 "Anne Frank," *Encyclopedia of World Biography*. Detroit: Gale, 1998.

12 Ibid.

13 Wilson, "My Diary," *My Secret Diary*, p. 1.

14 Ibid., "Clothes," p. 38.

15 Ibid., "My Diary," p. 10.

16 Ibid., "Writing," p. 118.

17 Ibid., p. 124.

18 Ibid., p. 125.

19 Ibid., p. 101.

20 Ibid., pp. 102–103.

21 Ibid., p. 103.

22 Ibid., p. 104.

23 Ibid., p. 108.

24 Ibid., p. 109.

25 Ibid., p. 110.

26 Ibid., "Books," p. 93.

27 Ibid., "Cornwall," p. 203.

28 Ibid., p. 204.

29 Ibid., p. 201.

30 Ibid., "Cookie," p. 224.

31 Ibid., p. 225.

32 Ibid., p. 239.

33 Ibid., p. 240.

34 Ibid., p. 241.

35 Ibid., p. 242.

36 Ibid., "School," p. 143.

37 Wilson, Bankston telephone interview.

38 Ibid.

Chapter 4

1 Wilson, "Chris," *My Secret Diary*, p. 43.

2 Ibid., p. 50.

3 Wilson, "Epilogue," *Jacky Daydream*, p. 346.

4 Ibid., p. 359.

5 Wilson, Bankston telephone interview.

6 Ibid.

7 Wilson, "Epilogue," *Jacky Daydream*, p. 359.

8 Ibid.

9 Ibid.

10 Ibid., p. 360.

11 Wilson, Bankston telephone interview.

12 Ibid.

13 Ibid.

14 "Jacqueline Wilson." http://www.amandacraig.com.

15 Wilson, Bankston telephone interview.

16 Ibid.

17 Greenstreet, "Wilson on *Jackie*."

18 Angela McRobbie, *Feminism and Youth Culture: From Jackie to Just Seventeen*, Boston: Unwin Hyman, 1991.

19 Ibid.

20 Ibid.

21 "Jacqueline Wilson," *Major Authors and Illustrators for Children and Young Adults*. Detroit: Gale, 2002.

Chapter 5

1 Edemarian, "Wilson: Grande Dame."

2 Wilson, Bankston telephone interview.

3 Ibid.

4 Ibid.

5 Edemarian, "Wilson: Grande Dame."

6 Wilson, Bankston telephone interview.

7 Judy Darley. "Children's and YA author Jacqueline Wilson Tells Us the Secrets of Writing for Young Readers." EssentialWriters.com.

http://essentialwriters.com/jacqueline-wilson-6100.htm.

8 Angelica Shirley Carpenter, "Drama Queen: Forget About Bambi, Thumper, and Flower. Jacqueline Wilson Writes About Domestic Violence, Mental Illness, and Parents Who Are Total Losers," *School Library Journal*. February 2006: p. 50+.

9 Ibid.

10 Wilson, Bankston telephone interview.

11 Ibid.

12 "Ed McBain," *Authors and Artists for Young Adults*. Vol. 39. Detroit: Gale, 2001.

13 Ibid.

14 Wilson, Bankston telephone interview.

15 Ibid.

16 Ibid.

17 "Wilson," Major Authors.

Chapter 6

1 Darley, "Wilson."

2 Wilson, Bankston telephone interview.

3 Steve Bowles, "Teenage Fiction—Another Uninspired Year," *Books for Keeps*, January, 1983.

4 K.L. Going, "History: Learning from the YA Past," *Writing & Selling the YA Novel*. Cincinnati: Writers Digest Books, 2008, p. 24.

5 Meg Cabot, "A Real Girl Loved by Girls Everywhere," *Shelf Discovery: The Teen Classics We Never Stopped Reading*. ed. Lizzie Skurnick. Fort Worth, Tex.: Avon, 2009, p. 52.

6 Carpenter, "Drama Queen," p. 50+.

7 Going, "History," *YA Novel*, p. 26.

8 "Wilson," *Major Authors*.

9 Wilson, Bankston telephone interview.

10 "Jacqueline Wilson." Contemporary Authors Online. http//www.gale.cengage.com/In Context/bio.htm.

11 Ibid.

12 Wilson, Bankston telephone interview.

13 Ibid.

Chapter 7

1 Sherry Garland, "The Writing Life Is It Worth It?" *Writing for Young Adults*. Cincinnati: Writer's Digest Books, 1998, p. 182.

2 Carpenter, "Drama Queen," p. 50.

3 Ibid.

4 "Nick Sharratt," Contemporary Authors Online.

5 Wilson, Bankston telephone interview.

6 Going, "Study Hall: Time to Delve into Authentic Teen Voice and Point of View," *YA Novel*, p. 120.

7 Jacqueline Wilson, *The Story of Tracy Beaker*. New York: Random House Children's, 1991, p. 8.

8 Ibid., p. 50.

9 Going, "Study Hall," *YA Novel*, p. 124.

10 Ilene Cooper, "The Story of Tracy Beaker, "*Booklist*, June 15, 2001: p. 1884.

11 Burnett, Frances Hodgson. *The Secret Garden*. Cambridge: Candlewick, 2010, p. 1.

12 Lizzie Skurnick, "Shut-in and Dig," *Shelf Discovery: The Teen Classics

We Never Stopped Reading*. Fort Worth, Tex.: Avon, 2009, p. 357.

13 "Wilson," *Major Authors*.

14 Wilson, Bankston telephone interview.

15 Ibid.

16 Carpenter, "Drama Queen," p. 50+.

17 Wilson, Bankston telephone interview.

18 Ibid.

19 Winifred Robinson, "The Very Hypocritical Ms. Wilson; Controversy: Jacqueline Wilson," (London) *Daily Mail*, March 5, 2008: p. 34.

20 Sue Corbett, "Jacky Who? A Household Name in the U.K., Jacqueline Wilson Tries for a Breakout in the States," *Publishers Weekly,* July 16, 2007: p. 33.

21 Wilson, Bankston telephone interview.

22 Robinson, "Ms. Wilson," p. 34. *Daily Mail.*

23 Wilson, Bankston telephone interview.

24 Ibid.

Chapter 8

1 Wilson, "Epilogue," *Jacky Daydream,* p. 346.

2 Ibid., p. 348.

3 Wilson, Bankston telephone interview.

4 Cooper, "Wilson, Illustrated Mum." *Booklist*, p. 862.

5 Carpenter, "Drama Queen," p. 50.

6 Wilson, Bankston telephone interview.

7 Ibid.

8 Ibid.

9 Liz O' Reilly. "Jacqueline Wilson." Contemporary Writers in the UK. http://www.contemporary writers.com/authors/?p=auth03d 16j381612635486.

10 Wilson, Bankston telephone interview.

11 "The British Invasion: PW Speaks to Five Authors Who Have Crossed the Atlantic and Found American Readers. (Children's Books)," *Publishers Weekly*, July 2002: p. 26.

12 Corbett, "Jacky Who?" p. 33.

13 "Candyfloss," *Publishers Weekly*, July 16, 2007: p. 165.

14 Corbett, "Jacky Who?", p. 33.

15 Wilson, Bankston telephone interview.

16 Ibid.

17 Ibid.

18 Edemarian, "Wilson: Grande Dame."

19 Wilson, Bankston telephone interview.

20 Ibid.

21 "Wilson." http://www.amandacraig. com.

22 Wilson, Bankston telephone interview.

23 Wilson, "Bournemouth," *Jacky Daydream*, pp. 343–344.

WORKS BY JACQUELINE WILSON

1972 *Hide and Seek*

1973 *Ricky's Birthday; Truth or Dare*

1974 *Snap*

1976 *Let's Pretend*

1977 *Making Hate*

1982 *Nobody's Perfect*

1983 *Waiting for the Sky to Fall*

1984 *The Killer Tadpole; The Other Side; The School Trip*

1985 *How to Survive Summer Camp*

1986 *Amber; The Monster in the Cupboard*

1987 *Glubbslyme; Lonely Hearts; Supersleuth; The Power of the Shade*

1988 *Rat Race; This Girl; Vampire*

1989 *Falling Apart; Is There Anybody There?: Volume 1—Spirit Raising; The Left Outs; The Party in the Lift*

1990 *Is There Anybody There?: Volume 2—Crystal Gazing; Take a Good Look*

1991 *The Dream Palace; The Story of Tracy Beaker; The Werepuppy*

1992 *Mark Spark; The Suitcase Kid; Video Rose*

1993 *Deep Blue; Mark Spark in the Dark; The Mum-Minder*

1994 *Come Back, Teddy!; Freddy's Teddy; Teddy at the Fair; Teddy Goes Swimming; The Bed and Breakfast Star; The Werepuppy On Holiday; Twin Trouble*

1995 *Cliffhanger; Double Act; Elsa, Star of the Shelter; Jimmy Jelly; Love from Katie; My Brother Bernadette; Sophie's Secret Diary; The Dinosaur's Packed Lunch*

1996 *Bad Girls; Beauty and the Beast; Connie and the Water Babies; Mr. Cool*

1997 *Girls in Love; The Lottie Project; The Monster Story-Teller*

1998 *Buried Alive!; Girls Under Pressure; Rapunzel*

1999 *Girls Out Late; Monster Eyeballs; The Illustrated Mum*

2000 *Lizzie Zipmouth*; *The Dare Game*; *Vicky Angel*

2001 *Dustbin Baby*; *Sleep-overs*; *The Cat Mummy*

2002 *Girls in Tears*; *Secrets*; *The Worry Website*

2003 *Lola Rose*; *Midnight*

2004 *Best Friends*; *The Diamond Girls*

2005 *Clean Break*

2006 *Candyfloss*; *Starring Tracy Beaker*

2007 *Jacky Daydream*; *Kiss*; *Totally Jacqueline Wilson*

2008 *Cookie*; *My Sister Jodie*; *Tracy Beaker Trilogy* (including *The Story of Tracy Beaker; The Dare Game*; and *Starring Tracy Beaker)*

2009 *Hetty Feather*; *My Secret Diary*

2010 *The Longest Whale Song*; *Little Darlings*

POPULAR BOOKS

GIRLS IN LOVE

The first in a four-part series, *Girls in Love* follows Elle as she competes with her friend's seemingly superior love life. She soon learns that the boy she has made up is better than the real ones her friends are dating.

HETTY FEATHER

Set in 1876 in London, the story begins when Hetty Feather's mother abandons the infant at the Foundling Hospital. This Victorian Tracy Beaker survives with a foster family and tries to find her birth mother.

HIDE AND SEEK

Jacqueline Wilson's first published novel follows the story of two kidnapped girls, their families, and the man who kidnapped them.

THE ILLUSTRATED MUM

Surviving her mother's slow descent into the grips of bipolar disorder, Dol does all she can to take care of her mother despite being 11 years old.

THE STORY OF TRACY BEAKER

Written as a journal kept by a young girl in a children's home, the novel manages to be both humorous and real, while Tracy tries to be a writer and find a family.

POPULAR CHARACTERS

DOL

In *The Illustrated Mum*, Dol, short for Dolphin, loves her tattooed Mom. She loves her mother although she is sometimes unhappy, or stays up all night, or drinks too much. But Dol worries that as her mother gets much worse, she will be put in an institution while Dol goes to foster care.

FLOSS

Deciding to stay with her father and his struggling chip business is a tough decision. After all, moving to Australia with her family would be more stable. But her dad *needs* her, and besides, life with dad may be unpredictable but it is also fun.

TRACY BEAKER

Rejected by her foster families, Tracy resolves to stay at The Children's Home until her real mother (who she is convinced is a famous Hollywood actress) rescues her, although she is willing to consider living with a messy writer until then.

MAJOR AWARDS

1995 Wins the Young Telegraph/Fully Booked Award for *The Bed and Breakfast Star*; Awarded the Nestlé Smarties Book Prize for *Double Act*.

1996 Wins the Sheffield Children's Book Award, *Double Act*.

1999 Shortlisted for the Whitbread Award for *The Illustrated Mum*.

2000 Wins London *Guardian* Children's Fiction Prize for *The Illustrated Mum*.

2002 Named to Order of the British Empire for services to literacy in schools.

2003 W.H. Smith Book Award (children's genre) for *Girls in Tears*.

2005 Named Britain's fourth Children's Laureate.

2007 Named as Dame Commander, Order of the British Empire.

BIBLIOGRAPHY

Books

Garland, Sherry. *Writing for Young Adults*. Cincinnati: Writer's Digest Books, 1998.

Going, K.L. *Writing & Selling the YA Novel*. Cincinnati: Writers Digest Books, 2008.

Goldberg, Natalie. *Writing Down the Bones: Freeing the Writer Within*. New York: Shambhala, 1986.

King, Stephen. *On Writing: A Memoir of the Craft*. New York: Pocket Books, 2000.

Lamott, Anne. *Bird by Bird*. New York: Anchor Books, 1994.

Skurnick, Lizzie. *Shelf Discovery: The Teen Classics We Never Stopped Reading*. New York: Avon, 2009.

Wilson, Jacqueline. *My Secret Diary: Dating, Dancing, Dreams and Dilemmas*. London: Corgi, 2009.

———. *Jacky Daydream*. New York: Doubleday UK, 2007.

Periodicals

Bowles, Steve. "Teenage Fiction—Another Uninspired Year," *Books for Keeps*, January, 1983.

"The British Invasion: PW Speaks to Five Authors Who Have Crossed the Atlantic and Found American Readers. (Children's Books)," *Publishers Weekly*, July 1, 2002: p. 26.

"Candyfloss," *Publishers Weekly*, July 16, 2007: p. 165.

Cooper, Ilene. "Wilson, Jacqueline. The Illustrated Mum." *Booklist*, January 1, 2005: p. 862.

———. "The Story of Tracy Beaker," *Booklist*, June 15, 2001: p. 1884.

Corbett, Sue. "Jacky Who? A Household Name in the U.K., Jacqueline Wilson Tries for a Breakout in the States," *Publishers Weekly*, July 16, 2007: p. 33.

Edemarian, Aida. "Jacqueline Wilson: the Grande Dame of Girlhood," (London) *Guardian,* July 10, 2010.

Greenstreet, Rosanna. "Jacqueline Wilson on *Jackie* Magazine," (London) *Guardian*, September 5, 2009, Culture section: p. 1.

Robinson, Winifred. "The Very Hypocritical Ms. Wilson; Controversy: Jacqueline Wilson," (London) *Daily Mail*, March 5, 2008: p. 34.

FURTHER READING

Books

Bradbury, Ray. *Zen in the Art of Writing*. Santa Barbara, Calif.: Capra Press, 1989.

Going, K.L. *Writing & Selling the YA Novel*. Cinncinati: Writers Digest Books, 2008.

Goldberg, Natalie. *Writing Down the Bones: Freeing the Writer Within*. New York: Shambhala, 1986.

King, Stephen. *On Writing: A Memoir of the Craft*. New York: Pocket Books, 2000.

Lamott, Anne. *Bird by Bird*. New York: Anchor Books, 1994.

Wilson, Jacqueline. *My Secret Diary: Dating, Dancing, Dreams and Dilemmas*. London: Corgi, 2009.

———. *Jacky Daydream*. New York: Doubleday UK, 2007.

Web Sites

Jacqueline Wilson
http://www.jacquelinewilson.co.uk

PICTURE CREDITS

INDEX

ABOUT THE CONTRIBUTOR

Born in Boston, Massachusetts, **JOHN BANKSTON** began writing articles while still a teenager. Since then, more than 200 of his articles have been published in magazines and newspapers across the country, including the *Tallahassee Democrat*, the *Orlando Sentinel*, and *The Tallahassean*. He is the author of more than 60 biographies for young adults, including works on scientist Stephen Hawking, anthropologist Margaret Mead, author F. Scott Fitzgerald, and actor Heath Ledger. He currently lives in Newport Beach, California.